# DOOMSDAY OR DETERRENCE?

# DOOMSDAY OR DETERRENCE?
## ON THE ANTINUCLEAR ISSUE

**FERENC FEHÉR**
**and**
**AGNES HELLER**

**M. E. SHARPE, INC.**
ARMONK, NEW YORK
LONDON, ENGLAND

Available in the United Kingdom and Europe from M. E. Sharpe,
Publishers, 3 Henrietta Street, London WC2E 8LU.

Published simultaneously as Vol. XVI, No. 1–2, of *International
Journal of Politics*

**Library of Congress Cataloging in Publication Data**

Fehér, Ferenc, 1933–
    Doomsday or deterrence

    1. Nuclear disarmament. 2. Antinuclear movement.
I. Heller, Agnes. II. Title.
JX1974.7.F38    1986      327.1'74      86-10074
ISBN 0-87332-368-8
ISBN 0-87332-369-6 (pbk.)

Printed in the United States of America

# Contents

# DOOMSDAY OR DETERRENCE?

# Introduction

*Doomsday or Deterrence* is a philosophico-political argument against the majority of the premises and conclusions of the current antinuclear movement and is intended as a contribution to an alternative politics of the democratic Left. This is, then, a *Gelegenheitsdichtung*, as Goethe put it, a piece written for an occasion, not an academic treatise.

Three major considerations guided us while writing this book. The first concerned the nature of the discourse we would participate in. This book was not written with the aim of furthering discussion concerning the technical and military dimensions of the debate over disarmament. We pretend to no expertise in such matters, although, of course, we do not deny their relevance to a debate characterized by polemics concerning the intentions, capabilities, or superiority of one side or the other. Nevertheless, we regard the predominance of military (mostly only pseudomilitary) jargon in present-day peace and antinuclear publications as a perversion of the discourse itself. There is nothing mystical about military technology as a branch of knowledge except the important fact that a crucial part of it remains secret. Moreover, deliberately false items of information are regularly leaked to the public "in the interest of national security." This fact is, however, sufficient to deprive military expertise of the most important feature of modern science: its public and generally controllable character. Further, in the pseudomilitary polemics in and around the antinuclear movement people usually preselect arguments and authorities that confirm their creeds rather than those that might undermine them. No amount of argument can convince the amateurish strategists of the eventual falsity of their idols. True, something similar often happens in "objective" and "scholarly" academic circles as well, but there exists in them, at least in principle, a certain kind of competence on the basis of which, and assuming scientific honesty, bias could be corrected. In the "military" polemics of the dilettanti of the antinuclear movement no such competence exists. It is religious creeds, often fairly fanatic ones impervious to rational arguments of any kind, that collide and conduct a pseudodialogue.

Our main objection to the "militarization" of the language of the antinuclear issue is our conviction that the danger, the existence of which would only be denied by fools, does not arise from technology of any kind, but from particular social dynamics. Therefore, it is our view that the discourse must remain on the level of ethical and political theory, and not on that of technology or pseudotechnology. If we wish to attain a world free of the danger and the fears of a global nuclear war, we have to achieve certain social changes that will curb the trends of technology, and not the other way round. Even the pathological growth of an apocalyptic-technological fantasy does more harm than good. To live constantly in a science-fiction world, under the shadow of a mushroom cloud, is little more than methodical self-education for collective hysteria.

The second major guiding principle of this book was our conviction that "the West," as the repository of democracy, is a value in itself that should be defended. We see the West as the copresence of three distinct dynamics: capitalism, industrialization, democracy, not a geographical concept. However, given that "the West" is the only world where there is democracy and, further, given that the antinuclear movement is a Western (West European and North American) phenomenon, it is entirely relevant to raise the imperative of defending the West precisely when the antinuclear movement is under scrutiny. The statement that "the West" is a value in itself has a double meaning. It is a value not only for those who conceive socialism as the radicalization of democracy, for whom, therefore, the democratic institutions of the West are necessary preconditions and constituents of a possible socialist future. Naturally, it is a value as well for liberals who do not intend the transcendence of the present state of affairs. Thus, there is a certain consensus concerning the value character of "the West" that is shared by almost everyone, even by the spiritual unilateralists. Precisely because of this very wide consensus, the fact of a mass defeatism represented by an important part of the antinuclear movements is one of the riddles this book has to solve.

Our third major consideration was that the great strategic interests and the objectives proper of socialism must remain primary as against the antinuclear trend. These days it is an almost religious belief in certain regions of the Left that the antinuclear movement is "objectively Leftist," or at least "objectively beneficial" to the Left. This is advocated in good faith and bad faith. It is advocated in good faith in the following terms: life comes first, freedom (or socialism or "social progress") can only come afterward. This is a position that we intend to show to be incorrectly formulated, leading to a fundamentally distorted communication in the antinuclear movement and based on false premises. Those who advocate the argument in bad faith, on the rare occasions they are ready to speak sincerely, will present the antinuclear movement as a new Trojan horse with which to achieve "some other" objective. Ironically, it is no longer Stalinist communists alone, the original inventors of the Trojan horse ploy, who resort to such language and practices. Many analysts have stated that the neonationalist current of the German antinuclear movement (which has absolutely nothing to do with communism of any kind even if it temporarily tolerates communists or *Nationalbolschewiks* among it) aims at a new Rapallo, a new status for Germany, while verbally struggling against the missiles. More recently, mainstream members of the Green Party have complained publicly about being used as a Trojan horse by Leftist manipulators. Precisely because we oppose all such practices for reasons of principle, we are also critical of a trend toward similar strategies detectable among East European dissidents. People with the most honorable convictions sometimes state, of course confidentially, that a peace (or antinuclear) movement could become instrumental in Eastern Europe in undermining the present systems of oppression. Apart from the fact that we believe this assumption (and the tactic based on it) illusory, we would warn all those who take seriously a possible future East European democracy against Trojan horse strategies of any kind. Most importantly, however, slogans like "life comes first, freedom afterward" demonstrate to us that the continuity with the movement of the sixties, with the latter's emphasis on freedom and the good life, has been severed. This book is intended as a contribution to the restoration of this continuity.

# I.   Life and Freedom as Universal Values of Modernity

The antinuclear movement is the movement par excellence of modernity in that its whole internal dynamic revolves, covertly or overtly, around the conflict of the only values of modernity that are *universal*: freedom and life. This conflict of values will be analyzed later. Here, we are more concerned with the exclusivity of freedom and life as universal, modern values in general.

The process of universalization, the end result of which is the exclusive position of the values of freedom and life, has several constituents. First, in the long process of the disintegration of communitarian and hierarchic worlds, a series of traditional values that had functioned as absolute at least within one or a few communities, and had been tendentially accepted in all of them (in that sense they had been almost general), have become relativized. *Loyalty*, a leading traditional value, is only the most conspicuous example. When for Juliet, Montague and Capulet are no longer valid points of reference, when Saint-Just declares that we have to be unfaithful in order to be free, when Jews become emancipated by voluntarily leaving the ritual community, when Lenin incites to civil war against the war of one's own country, and Sorge betrays the Fatherland for the world proletariat and humankind, to mention examples entirely different in character and value content, then disloyalty can be chosen as a value and loyalty is no longer universal. Second, certain typically modern values, close competitors of freedom and life, lost out in the race and never attained a universal status. Two such values, equality and reason, occupying a distinguished position in all Enlightenment projects, stand out quite forcefully. Of them, we shall only briefly analyze equality because of its overwhelming political significance.

Equality and inequality are not natural propensities; persons are unique and incommensurable. Equality and inequality are constituted by norms and rules. People belonging to the same social cluster are socially equal in that the same norms and rules apply to them. We can, and should, claim that humankind ought to be the overarching social cluster, but only on the condition that the common norms and rules be such as to diminish, or eventually abolish, domination, force, and violence. Put simply, the common norms and rules constituting the overarching essential social cluster should ensure *freedom*.

The claim for equality is therefore subjected to the claim for freedom. In other words, equality is not an ultimate value. Whenever people claim equality, they claim equality in something. This "something" can have entirely different meanings, but all of them can be reduced to two all-encompassing ones: equality in freedom(s) and equality in life-chances (termed during the Jacobin period *égalité de fait*). The claim for equality of freedom can encompass two claims, and both can be related to two interpretations of freedom. The first claim is one for equal *rights*, the second is one for equal *possibilities* to practice those rights. The first interpretation of freedom is the democratic, the second is the liberal. (Isaiah Berlin termed them "positive" freedom and "negative" freedom respectively.) One can claim that each person should have equal rights to participate in all decision-making processes affecting his or her community or body politic; one can further claim that each person should have equal rights to and equal possibilities of the same participation. The claim to the possibility of practicing freedoms (both positive and negative) combines the claim to equality of freedom and of life-chances. All such claims can be brought under the following formula: The norms and rules of society should be such as to ensure the right (eventually the possibility) of each and every one to participate in all decision-making processes affecting their community or body politic (the pursuit of public happiness). As a consequence, all norms and rules, whatever social cluster they may constitute, should ensure the same. Further, the norms and rules of society should be such as to ensure the right (eventually the possibility) for each and every one to decide upon his or her fate, to choose his or her form of life.

It is obvious that equality in freedom and equality in life do not contradict one another. It is also obvious that equality is not regarded here as an independent universal value, but rather as the condition for the complete and unfailing observance of freedom and life. However, even if on the level of logic there is no contradiction between equality in freedom and equality in life chances (for we can claim norms and rules that encompass both), in reality there are such contradictions. It is this circumstance that triggered the attempt to raise equality to the level of a universal value of modernity, even the claim that it should be the supreme value. Indeed, in this attempt *égalité de fait* was interpreted as the factual equality of all (and not as the equality of life-chances). But *égalité de fait* is a self-contradictory concept for it excludes equality of freedom in that it denies that all persons are (ontologically) unique and incommensurable, and therefore it includes, implicitly or explicitly, the project of a dictatorship over needs, values, and opinions. *Quod erat demonstrandum*: equality is not a universal value for it is conditional, not unconditional.

There has hardly ever been a culture in which *life,* at least in some respects, would not have constituted a value. A whole culture based on "being-toward-death" is inconceivable as a lasting state of affairs. *Freedom*, once again in some respects, has always been a value (for example, as the freedom of the citizen of the city-state or the republic). At the same time, in each and every pre-Enlightenment period neither freedom nor life constituted general values. For no free and republican Roman, favoring the expansion of Rome, did it make sense to speak of the freedom of the slaves or of conquered realms. And Marx correctly termed a whole, later, period of European history the democracy of *unfreedom*, from which it clearly follows that in fundamental aspects of its social organization, freedom could not be claimed as a general, not to mention universal, value. Similarly, in certain respects cultures have always denied individuals or groups the right to life. We have in mind several forms of human sacrifice, the "superfluous" lives of the weak, the old, the newborn female, the unprotected lives of the heathen or the alien, natural targets of persecution, the life of the body as against that of the soul (the former was often to be shed in order for the latter to be perpetuated in accordance with a value preference). In several cultures suicide was absolutely prohibited, but in several others, at least for certain members of the ruling elite and in extreme situations, it was acceptable, commendable, or simply required, and in no way optional. The universalizing process taking place from the early eighteenth century onward, and covering the whole period of the Enlightenment, always had recourse to natural right theory, and it sometimes stressed freedom, and at other times life, as primary universal values. (For instance, in Hobbes's conception, the commonwealth can limit freedom as a value, but not life; when life is no longer respected in all respects, that is to say, as a universal value, man relapses into a state of nature.) In a later eighteenth-century development, recourse was rather made to freedom as a universal value. Indeed, one could legitimately argue that whenever one value had been universalized, the universalizing process of the other was well under way. Thus, the two great documents heralding the birth of modernity, the American Declaration of Independence and the French Declaration of Man and Citizen, stress, as the starting point of all social and political discourse, the right to life *and* freedom as universal values.

Freedom and life have become *value ideas* of modernity. This implies that while they can be and indeed are infringed daily, their opposites cannot be publicly and validly chosen as values. Their predominant position is partly derivative of, partly well-established in, the three logics of modernity, capitalism, industrialization, and the political process toward democracy. This can be seen in three ways. First, one of the modern logics, the process aiming at democracy, supports *both* freedom and life; in a sense, democracy is nothing but the institutionalization of the universal rights to (or values of) life and freedom. Second, the other two dynamics can support one of the universal values while being hostile to the other. For instance, both capitalism and industrialization can be hostile to life, can in a popular sense "exploit" life. Thus, if we look at the frighteningly low life expectancy of the early capitalist, industrializing period, we can see that this assertion is more than a metaphor.

Capitalism and industrialization, however, are not necessarily hostile to freedom either in a partial or in a universal sense. Finally, none of the three logics is intrinsically incompatible with the universalized values of life and freedom, while both *martial cultures* and the systems of *personal dependence*, the longest lasting form of domination in human history, necessarily are.

The simultaneous ascendancy of life and freedom to the rank of universal values does not mean that conflicts and collisions between them—in a theoretical or practical form—are inconceivable. Just the contrary. The whole, short history of modernity is full of such conflicts and polemics in which there are different levels of the discussion, and the problem invariably raised in the discussions is not that of validity (both are simultaneously and incessantly posited as values), but that of priority. The three levels of value conflicts between life and freedom are a) the everyday level, b) the level of nation, class, and other higher integrations, and c) the level of humankind. In this book we shall disregard the highly important everyday level of value discussions and shall concentrate on the other two levels. Even if, however, we assume the existence of a third level, that of humankind, on which the coexistence of life and freedom as universal values is a valid and recognized social fact, the process cannot be regarded as entirely completed yet. It is not so much Nazism that we have in mind, but rather the Islamic-fundamentalist revival in which the value of freedom is outright problematical and, as the Islamic cult of self-sacrifice demonstrates, the value of life has remained very relative indeed. Conflicts around the priority of one or the other value can be best exemplified, first, by the problem of suicide and, secondly, by the abolition of the prerogatives of *pater familias* over the lives of the members of his household. Suicide as a right means, *ipso facto*, the priority of freedom over life; the abolition of certain paternal rights means the priority of life over (a certain kind of) freedom.

The modern concept of barbarism can be understood as more meaningful than an exercise in journalese precisely on this basis. Whereas discussions concerning the priority of one or other of the universal values of life and freedom are ''normal,'' ''functional'' tensions of modernity, and whereas an all-out conflict between the two is a dangerous signal of an overt or covert crisis, as well as an index of the latent inhumanity of our culture, tensions or conflicts do not imply the withdrawal of recognition from the two universal values. Barbarism, however, means the explicit or implicit denial of the universal value character of both, or occasionally of one of them. The qualification (explicit or implicit) here is necessary. Nazism became the *negative paradigm* precisely by committing the same (or closely similar) atrocities as Stalin, while the Nazi leaders stated their aims (or a considerable number of them) publicly, and Stalin's regime went through elaborate efforts aimed at covering the same crimes with a facade of ''socialist humanism.'' There is no need to comment on how Hitler's necrophile revolution ''revalued'' the universal values of freedom. Nor is it necessary to analyze what kind of value the Nazis attributed to others' lives. The necrophile attitude, however, was consistent. Hitler's almost naive question, when the endangered life of the German youth was mentioned in connection with the further pursuit of his doomed war, ''Does it matter when we die?'' and his determination to pull the whole of Germany into his tomb in an ultimate act of *Götterdämmerung* amply testify to this consistency. Of course, all analysts of Stalin's peculiar way of waging war know perfectly well that the Generalissimo (who was a sadist but not a necrophile) felt exactly the same indifference toward the fate of his soldiers; millions of Soviet casualties fell victim to this indifference. However, for reasons that point far beyond the differences between the personal psychologies of the fuehrers, this could not be made a public principle (although it was a guiding maxim of practice) in the Soviet regime. This is, however, merely a matter of difference between the various paradigms of barbarism. The socially relevant fact is that the abolition of only one of the universal values is sufficient to make a system utterly barbarous.

The essence of modern culture would be missed, were one to regard the obvious tension between the genocides regularly committed under its aegis, sometimes even on an unprecedented scale, and the recognition of the universal values of freedom and life by a social consensus as mere hypocrisy. It is precisely this duality, this tragic tension, that provokes the constant efforts at redefining the permissible, respectively impermissible, measure of collective violent acts, which occasionally brings into being punitive authorities, in themselves incompatible with the rules of the game set by this civilization. The Nuremberg "court" which had indeed almost no formal legal basis and hardly any other basis but the universal values of life and freedom was one such instance. The tension also triggers attempts at the synthesis of life and freedom. As to the constant redefinition of the measure of permissible collective violent acts, the very need for defining the permissible degree would have been inconceivable for men of several premodern cultures: "dog eat dog" was a practically unquestioned maxim in most of them. So was, in certain circumstances, genocide, as can be seen in a civilization, otherwise so refined, such as the Roman at the conclusion of the Punic wars. It is an untenable prejudice, against which the hecatombes erected by Ghengis Khan or Tamerlane argue with vigor, that genocide was invented by modernity. It was only the *negative concept* of genocide based on the universal value of life that can be attributed to modernity as an invention, an invention which provokes the condemnation of modernity as hypocritical but which makes it possible to pronounce moral judgment, occasionally to effect sanctions in the name of the ethico-political justice. In earlier periods, only Cassandra's raving despair would have been conceivable. The basis of such judgments is the restoration of the good life (the condition of which is the unification of the universal values of life and freedom) to its central place in a possible modern ethic.

Modern life is full of value conflicts between freedom and life. Of these and in preparation for the discussion of these conflicts in the antinuclear movement we only mention two: the conflict of life and freedom in recent Christian conceptions and in modern revolutionary, or socialist, consciousness. As to the first, we are obviously dealing in abstractions. Despite recent ecumenical trends, there is still no unified "Christian" theology. With their usual flexibility, Christian theologies adjust to the new situation created by the "loss of legitimacy of Western capitalism," which simply means that capitalism has ceased to be a "natural state of affairs." Churches could have reacted to this new constellation (which was accompanied in Europe, but not in the United States, by a considerable weakening of religious fervor) in accordance with both universal values, freedom and life. In a way, they have. All churches have shifted their previous, almost unconditional support for ultraconservative regimes toward a defense of human rights (in particular in Latin America). For a number of reasons not to be analyzed here,* however, it is more natural if in religious conceptions priority is given to life as against freedom. The sanctity of life, with certain important provisos and exceptions, has traditionally been a value for all Christian theories and theologies.† The majority of Protestant churches have become in the last decades, in Scandinavia and in the Anglo-Saxon world, ardent supporters and employees of the welfare state, with all its excessive emphasis on life. The shock of Hitlerism pushed the churches further toward an emphasis on human life as a universal value (this time almost without qualification).

An overt or covert fundamentalism in Christian churches, bent on regaining their lost or weakened influence, also recommends such a stance. In several major conflicts in everyday discourse, such as abor-

---

*Freedom has traditionally had a restricted, metaphysical-ontological status in religion, that of our *moral* freedom to choose between good and bad, which hardly ever had derivatives (except the important Protestant postulate of the freedom of religious practices) in the field of political theory. The well-known fact that certain religious trends and sects served as vehicles of movements that are regarded in retrospect as emancipatory is an entirely different problem. The religious pathos in defense of human rights is a problem for Christian theories rather than a "natural conclusion."

†Even here, however, consistent Christians understand how inauthentic it is for a true Christian to be tragically concerned about Doomsday, nuclear or otherwise. The archbishop of York rightly stated the following: "This debate is about the end of the world and about how we may best prevent it or delay it. Of course this is in remarkable contrast with our founders in the historic Church who fervently longed for the end of the world and eagerly awaited it." See the important document, "The Church and the Bomb," *Proceedings of the General Synod*, vol. 14, no. 1, London, February 1983.

tion, the unreserved defense of life (or a maximalistic definition of what life is) strengthens the fundamentalist positions. All this is not to say that we are simply facing shrewd manipulators in certain dignitaries of the churches, for they never act *entirely* against their own principles. If now, in the antinuclear debate, several dignitaries of various Christian churches declare the nuclear deterrent immoral regardless of the political consequences of unilateralism (for instance, the American Catholic bishops do, the majority of the dignitaries of the Church of England do not), those condemning it act, at least in one respect, according to their traditions. Overall political freedom has never belonged to the main concerns of Christian bureaucracies. In a way, they do what they regard as correct (with a certain but not excessive amount of self-hypnosis and glossing over of several inner contradictions in their theories), and they follow interests they regard as vital for Christians. What we would like to state here in anticipation is not that the church dignitaries are shrewd operators but that the marriage of their present "religion of life" and the Leftist positions is unnatural.

A similar discussion as to which of the two universal values should have priority takes place on the Left. This of course has a very lengthy prehistory which can only be sketched here, not analyzed in detail. Originally, on the socialist or revolutionary Left (the two concepts are obviously not identical), not only were both life and freedom regarded as universal values, but it is fair to say that it was precisely socialism, together with its major partner in polemics, liberalism, that advocated them as universal. However, priorities have constantly shifted. In the first half of the nineteenth century, life (in the form of the defense of the life of the worker against capitalist exploitation) had an almost absolute priority. Freedom, in states where the electorate, the number of *practically* free citizens, had almost everywhere been reduced to the well-off, was the rich man's prerogative and concern. The working man fought, above all, against his or her frighteningly low life expectancy. The golden age of socialist thought, from the Paris Commune to the First World War, reconciled the two fundamental values in an extremely harmonious way: freedom was a value in itself for the self-organizing proletariat and at the same time the natural vehicle for safeguarding life. But that did not prove to be a stable equilibrium. When in the cataclysms of World War One the myth of freedom became the dominant revolutionary socialist ideology (in the form of Bolshevism), a deeply problematic polarization took place. Practical communist ethics demanded contempt for life: for one's own, and even more for those of others, the "enemies." Allegedly all this happened in the name of freedom. What kind of freedom this priority discussion brought about, a discussion that bordered on the *theoretical* renouncement of life as a universal value, is too well-known to be commented on. By way of a reaction, in social democracy there was a timid emphasis on life, with justified hostility to terrorism, but with such an excessive caution that sometimes social democratic leaders, like Otto Bauer, felt, not incorrectly, that the excessive emphasis on life was instrumental in losing the possibilities for freedom. After World War Two, the New Left made an attempt at restoring the equilibrium by advocating freedom in the form of de-alienation, which was at least meant as the good life. But in fact, freedom (in a form totally different from its Bolshevik myth) gained the upper hand to an extent that in several different respects there emerged an almost overt contempt for life, from "revolutionary" self-sacrifice to the sacrificing of others. The cult of drugs, an unexpected development in the traditionally nonhedonistic Left, was an important proof of this. The ideology was centered on "peak experience," the direct sensation of life as totality, the disregard of time, life duration included.

In the 1970s, mostly under the impact of the deep recession, though also as a result of several other factors, the New Left ideology and movement disintegrated and the Bolshevik hostility to pacifism, its unmitigated harshness toward human life became largely discredited. (The last chapter of this "great disillusionment" was the loss of faith in Maoism.) This collapse left social discourse in a state of such disarray that nowadays it is only conducted with balance and realism on the everyday level. Almost all questions that are discussed from day to day, irrespective of the solutions we might occasionally reject, are addressed to the *simultaneous recognition* of life and freedom as universal values. In the vehement discussion of abortion the embryo's existence, defined as life, is contrasted with women's freedom of control over their bodies, and generally over their lives. In the newly arisen problem of whether a patient (or in case of the patient's irreversibly comatose state, his or her closest relatives) can have the right to decide on the withdrawal of life-sustaining mechanisms, the conflict of life and freedom is just as clear as their mutual recognition in their capacity as unquestionable values. In animal liberation, parasitic as this predilection in the present world of human suffering might seem, we face a hypostatizing of life as a universal value that is immediately translated into the language of freedom with certain inherent conflicts between the two. (Thus arises the question of whether, even if vegetarianism were to become consensually accepted, human life could be sustained under the consumption of meat.) Personal habits and industrial practices that are regarded as health hazards raise *ipso facto* the conflict, as well as the mutual recognition, of life and freedom as universal values.

In the all-embracing discourse concerning the allegedly impending nuclear holocaust that so inundates academia, the television screen, and newspapers alike, *the global conflict of life and freedom has reached the level of antinomy.* As a result, both freedom and life tend to lose their universal value character: an antinomy is an antinomy precisely because neither pole can be chosen against the other, and something that cannot be chosen is hardly a universal value. However, there is a graver danger: the self-barbarization of our culture. On the one hand, freedom cannot be opted for against life in a general sense, however much we despise the type Castoriadis has justly called "human zoologists." This is so for the simple reason that where there is no life "in general," there is no freedom either. All those who conceive the Bomb to be anything other than a deterrent, that is to say, who consider it a weapon with which an all-out war *should* be fought, however freedom-loving their motives might be, theoretically destroy freedom, as well as morality. What is beyond humanity is cosmological, not moral. It suffices to accept this alternative as more or less inevitable to undermine the moral pillars of our position. On the other hand, when *life is globally opted for against freedom in the form of mere survival*, regardless of what sort of life it would be in a world bereft of freedom, the good life is no longer possible, life is not worth living, and the choice is not more, rather much less moral than the former. This is more than a hypothetical assumption. Alun Chalfont* quotes several cases of writers (Auberon Waugh, E. P. Thompson) who expressly advocate this side of the alternative. Generally speaking, all partisans of the formula "better Red than dead" share the same position. Before commencing a political discussion of this position, three points should be made. Those who advocate a surrender to the Soviet nuclear threat (and from the context it is clear that, whatever the formulation, it is precisely this threat they have in mind) speak of something temporary, something that will "pass away." Apart from their word, however, there is no guarantee whatsoever to ensure that it is not the final establishment of a worldwide dictatorship that is being recommended in the name of survival. Further, the partisans of this formula obviously recommend surrender to everyone, otherwise their recommendation would make

---

*"The Great Unilateralist Illusion," *Encounter* (April 1983).

no sense, and the clash between the antagonists would remain inevitable. But how can it be ensured that everyone would prefer mere survival in a way of life that is intolerable for many to a life that many of those who oppose surrendering consider to be incomparably more meaningful, if not by the extermination of the partisans of "a meaningful life?" In other words, survival is ensured not in the name of life in general, but in the name of a voluntarily accepted or coercively imposed unfreedom. The formula "better Red than dead" puts freedom and life necessarily on a collision course, thereby destroying both as universal values. The assumption is that, if worst comes to worst, *everyone must become Red*, and the dissenters threaten everyone else with destruction. Therefore, if need be, dissenters must be wiped out, and therefore neither life in general nor freedom serves as a universal value any longer. Finally, in the light of the GULAG, Kampuchea, and the Chinese hecatombs (more recently, in Tibet), how can anyone guarantee, or even simply promise, that even a consensually peaceful surrender to a global Soviet nuclear threat will not imply the destruction of gigantic clusters of victims whose survival is going to be deemed superfluous, or even pernicious, by the triumphant new order?* There are no answers, and indeed there can be no answers to these questions from a position that opts globally for life, against freedom "if need be." This is the option of the self-imposed barbarization of Western civilization.

If the two universal values appear in an irreconcilable, antinomic form in vast social movements, however, the cause cannot be "misunderstanding," "slipshod formulation," or even the "shrewd manipulation" of certain ideologues. Rather, the cause must be deep-rooted and social in character. E. P. Thompson deserves credit for having first formulated the problem with such a broad historico-sociological relevance:

---

*Recently, there have been widely publicized mass executions carried out in China, allegedly as a deterrent against crime waves. If we for some reason believe the authorities, it is only criminals who are being executed, perpetrators of such crimes as "theft and hooliganism." If we believe them, the authorities have surely committed a heinous crime, in a country the leaders of which solemnly declared only recently that the murderous days of the Cultural Revolution would never return. But there is no reason to believe them; the Dalai Lama has already warned that political dissidents are being dealt with by execution squads, and there is very good reason to assume that the unruly youths full of oppositional sentiments are the real target. Nor is there reason to believe the numbers indicated by them: "only" 5,000 executed, "only" 50,000 deported to camps for an indefinite time. And what can the advocates of the formula "better Red than dead" guarantee us in the light of all this? Perhaps the well-known tranquilizer of our youth: *bei uns in Deutschland* things like that cannot happen?

The Bomb is, after all, something more than an inert Thing. First, it is, in its destructive yield and in its programmed trajectory, a thing of menace. Second, it is a component in a weapons-*system*: and producing, manning and supporting that system is a correspondent social system—a distinct organization of labour, research and operation, with distinctive hierarchies of command, rules of secrecy, prior access to resources and skills, and high levels of policing and discipline: a distinctive organization of production, which, while militarist in character, employs and is supported by great numbers of civilians (civil servants, scientists, academics) who are subordinated to its discipline and rules. . . . There is an internal dynamic and reciprocal logic here which requires a new category for its analysis. If "the handmill gives you society with the feudal lord; the steam-mill, society with the industrial capitalist", what are we given by those Satanic mills which are now at work, grinding out the means of human extermination? I have reached this point of thought more than once before, but have turned my head away in despair. Now, when I look at it directly, I know that the category which we need is that of 'exterminism.'*

For several reasons, we would use a different kind of conceptualization; we work with the terms capitalism, industrialization, and the political process aiming at democracy. The one at work here is the industrializing dynamic, or logic, which set free scientific thinking as an unlimited enterprise, and which promoted Enlightenment but now has reached a level where there is the very real threat that Enlightenment might be revoked altogether. This is, much more than anything else stressed in the famous book by Adorno and Horkheimer, what we regard as the negative dialectic of Enlightenment; this is what has been called by Solzhenitsyn the "New Fall."† This is a "negative dialectic" in the strictest sense of the word. Industrialism was invented as man's best "progress-making" tool; the very term suggests something morally and socially commendable. Industrialism—in its unlimited, that is, ideal form—created, for the first time in human history, the perfect means for complete human self-destruction. Industrial civilization is the first potentially suicidal civilization. This is the first set of "negative dialectical contradictions," which presuppose and comple-

---

*E. P. Thompson, *Zero Option* (London: Merlin Press, 1982), p. 45.

†Solzhenitsyn is absolutely consistent when he attacks Sakharov, whose moral greatness he is always ready to praise, the scientist who had the moral courage to turn against his own invention and lose his status and privileges, but who had not had foresight enough to "burn the drawings," the infernal design. Clearly, in this presentation Sakharov's responsibility is not personal but symbolic; he represents Unlimited Science, the enterprise par excellence of the Faustian Man.

ment one another. The second set is the following. The industrializing dynamic has put "instrumental rationalism" at the pinnacle of its leading principles. Instrumental rationalism literally means following the rationality (or logic) of the instruments we have produced; in hypostatizing them, one can predict the growth that is "progress"; all other principles are either false or moralizing poetry. This indeed has proved to be a victorious principle of the irresistible momentum of industrialization. It contained in itself, however, neither the principles for the moral limitation of this dynamic (and therefore no principle preventing us from forging the means for self-destruction) nor the principles ensuring the good life; nor, finally, the principles that would have ensured life itself. The report of the Club of Rome was only the first to foretell (realistically or not—in this respect it makes no difference) that unlimited industrialization will destroy life.

A traditional Marxist objection to this would be that separating, even for the sake of a theoretical argument, the problem of capitalism from that of industrialization and presupposing two distinct logics raises the question as to why capitalist industrialization has assumed this suicidal course. But we do not think that a traditional Marxist analysis can untangle this mystery any more than we can. The most obvious explanation, namely, that war (and preparation for war) is "profit making," an explanation which would account for what is happening to our civilization by the profit rate of the American military-industrial complex, has already been criticized by Mary Kaldor in her interesting and original article "Warfare and Capitalism." There she emphasizes that the "mode of warfare" is never a simple "reflection" of a "mode of production" and, further, that profit making is not an entirely successful explanation given that in one sense war is the diametrical opposite of capitalist production: it is destructive, not (value) productive. Her explanation, that American capitalism, being in a generalized state of crisis (in the analysis of which she is in broad agreement with the theory of Immanuel Wallerstein), seeks a "symbolic legitimation" through preparation for a war that in fact is not to be fought, is an ingenious theory but fraught, we believe, with one ultimate blindness. She writes: "Continued preparations for war . . . is, I would argue, designed to impress European and Third World states as much as the Soviet Union. . . . As domestic US capital and labour suffer the effects of imperialist competition, undermining both the fiscal basis and legitimacy of the American state, the enemy seems somehow to get displaced and blame is accorded to the Soviet Union. *Deterrence can be viewed as a kind of* *imaginary replay of World War II,* in which the Soviet Union plays the role of Nazi Germany and the United States 'saves' Europe.''* The conception of ''seeking symbolic legitimation'' for a shattered capitalist world power is only seemingly less orthodox than the usual explanation that is offered. The quotation marks placed around the word ''saves'' not only indicate a definite political position (namely, that the Soviet Union does not threaten Europe, or that ''Sovietization'' is not a danger), but also display the very traditional Marxist view that the problem of democracy is not something distinct, but a mere ''superstructural phenomenon.''

By contrast, we believe that the Bomb, this Thing, as E. P. Thompson correctly calls it, is a system, a *juncture of human-social relations,* and one which demonstrates all three logics of modernity in a conflictual interplay. It is only in this complexity that the Bomb, the antinuclear issue, can be understood as the crossroad and field of conflict of the two universal values of modernity. It is only in this complexity, and not by reducing all to one explanatory factor alone, that we can grasp the dangers we are facing. The logic of industrialization, which, once launched, no longer tolerates limitation (except in a society that could legitimately be called socialist), is one of the explanations of the arms race, in both world systems. (This in itself should justify not tying the problem to capitalism alone.) Second, in the West there are several factors implicating the Bomb with the direct and indirect interests of American and world capitalism. Such factors are, among others, the profit making of the gigantic (primarily American) military-industrial complex, the American ''quest for symbolic legitimation'' (Mary Kaldor's thesis), the heightened rearmament cycle as a stimulant to capitalist production in deep depression,† and the role of American capitalism as the guardian of world capitalism. But thirdly, *the defense of Western democracy* (saving which, without quotation marks, has been attributed for decades to the United States by the party to which Mary Kaldor belongs), is an equally important factor for the explanation of all those who would see not socialist progress but rather a catastrophe in the Sovietization of Europe, and who do not believe such a perspective to be mere childish daydreaming. It is only against this complex background that we can fully understand the clash between freedom and life

*Mary Kaldor, ''Warfare and Capitalism,'' in *Exterminism and Cold War,* ed. New Left Review (London: Verso, 1982), pp. 261–62.

†This is the argument of Paul Piccone and Victor Zaslavsky in ''The Socio-Economic Roots of Re-armament,'' *Telos* 50 (1981–82), pp. 5–18.

as universal values in the antinuclear movement.

All this makes mandatory the reconsideration of Grotius's dilemma: the *right* to war and peace, the problem of "just" and "unjust" war. We follow closely this classic treatise with some modifications. The latter stem from the shift of values that has taken place between Grotius's time and ours, from the changes in the technological means of warfare, and finally from the fact that certain social problems, then extremely important, have in the meantime become irrelevant. While these days there is almost a consensus that "old theories are old hat" and do not provide us with answers in our extreme need, we, by contrast, believe that this modern world is only comprehensible if we start from the old, which continues to exist in the present one. Finally, it is a fact that for forty years now, we have been living in this so-called peace in an uninterrupted chain of wars which are neither nuclear nor global, and which therefore must be understood in terms of an updated traditional theory. It is on this traditional basis, and on no other, that nuclear and nonnuclear world wars threaten us.

What is a "just" (as opposed to an "unjust") war? Is there a "right" to war? Why do we relate wars to justice and not to some other ethical category? While this century has seen the promulgation of certain international agreements that function as formal legal statutes and stipulations (such as the Geneva convention concerning the treatment of prisoners of war or the ban on chemical weapons), they are not sufficient in number, for various reasons generally not recognized by every state, and they do not cover all instances of the starting, waging, and concluding of wars. Further, there is little hope that such consensually accepted agreements can be promulgated in sufficient number. Therefore, it would be unnecessary to deny that we have recourse in our theory to a certain, streamlined version of natural law. (Recourse to updated natural law, as already stated, also lay at the basis of the Nuremberg Trial.) It differs from the traditional religious and lay conceptions of natural law, which also deal with the problem of the right to war, insofar as the basis of this streamlined version is the recognition of life and freedom as universal values.

Wars are, then, regarded as a special case of value conflicts (which regularly occur in human life), more precisely of *conflict between the two universal values*. In such a conflict, freedom and life are recognized as values (otherwise it would be meaningless to speak of their conflict); further, they appear either as a conflict between life and freedom, or as a conflict between the various interpretations of freedom, or as a conflict between the various interpretations of life. In each and every conflict, we have to determine priorities, either by action or by abstention from action. Both action and abstention have to be justified. Justification has to be public and made in such a way that those justifying their acts have to assume that everyone accepts (or can accept) their justification, even where this may not actually be the case. The very procedure of justification and the fact that a "just war" is conceived as an act of reconstituting a state that has been violated and upset by an unjust act are the explanation for why we relate wars to the concept of justice and call them "just" or "unjust." However, because just acts of war are justified as actions related to values (not to imperative norms), the form of justifying (the act of war, the act of starting or waging war) cannot assume the following form: "You must do so because. . . . " It can only be formulated in the following manner: "What I do is *permissible* because it is just, for the following consideration." There is, therefore, no just war that one must start or wage in obedience to an external and absolute norm; at most, it is permissible to do so. As a result, even in deciding whether or not a just war should be waged, pragmatic considerations (for instance, the collective recognition of the fact that, however just our case, we shall perish if we start a war, or if we resist) always play an important role. At the same time, it has to be stressed that both action and abstention from action have serious moral consequences and have to be assessed morally.

Classifying wars into the clusters "just" and "unjust" relies on three standards: the right to war, the conduct of war, and the character of peace at the conclusion of a war. In an ultimate abstraction, the relation between the three factors is the following. Without a right to war there can be no just war. An initial just cause, which can be absolute and relative, is a *conditio sine qua non* of a just war. Even a just cause, however, can lose degrees of its just character through the unjust conduct of war; similarly, the just conduct of war does not make the war just without an initial, just cause. Finally, if there was an initial, just cause (a right to war), if the war was conducted in a just manner, but the conditions of peace that the parties accept to conclude the war are unjust, either the war loses, in retrospect, its just character or at least the unjust conclusion reveals, again in retrospect, that the initial cause was contradictory. The motive of justice cannot have exhausted the ensemble of the objectives of war; there must have been other unjust goals as well. The formulation makes an important fact visible to the attentive reader. While we regard the first factor (the initial just cause) as absolute (both in its absolute and relative form), we regard the second and the third as relative. The conduct of war is relative because it is not determined by the considerations and intentions of one party alone, but is codetermined by the deeds of an enemy fighting an unjust war. (On the contrary, it is entirely within our power not to launch an unjust war based on an unjust initial cause.) The conduct of war is also relative in that there are degrees of its just and unjust character; generally in a war the two components blend. Almost all partisan armies, from the Spanish guerilla against Napoleon to Tito's glorious partisan *armada* (which are, legally speaking, regular armies fighting for the reconquest of dispossessed national sovereignty), fight, as a rule, with terrible methods. They acknowledge no prisoners of war; mass executions and setting whole towns on fire are regular features of their warfare. However, this is always determined or codetermined by a situation created by an invading enemy; here as well there is a consideration of degrees. We know from Kopelew's descriptions that the Soviet Army in East Prussia (and elsewhere) killed many innocent German women, children, old people; this was indeed a terrible crime which detracted a good deal from their otherwise deserved war glory.* However, as long as it did not develop into a methodical mass extermination of whole clusters of the populace (which characterized the German methods in Poland and the Ukraine), such conduct of war diminished but certainly did not destroy the just character of its war.

An unjust peace also admits of degrees of injustice. If it finalizes the power prerogatives of the victor over the vanquished (as happened, with or without peace treaties, in the case of the Soviet Union and Eastern Europe), it reveals the contradictory character of the initial war

---

*A full portrayal of the horrors committed by Soviet Army personnel, Soviet and local secret police, local militias, and the like against German civilian population in Silesia, East Prussia, Czechoslovakia, Rumania, Yugoslavia, and Hungary in the last months of the war and its immediate aftermath, a practice to be further pursued in certain areas for years, can be found in Theodor Schieder, ed., *Dokumentation der Vertreibung der Deutschen aus Ost-Mitteleuropa* (Documents of the Expulsion of Germans from East Central Europe), 8 vols. (Munich: DTV, 1984). This collective Calvary of roughly twelve million people which in all probability resulted in the loss of some two million lives caused by mass deportations, indiscriminate killing and organized mass executions, manmade famine, and epidemic diseases, far beyond the inevitable hardships of postwar decay, cannot be exonerated in any way. This is so even if we take into consideration the undeniable political responsibility of German ethnic groups in the respective countries for having supported Hitler's colonizing policies, as well as the Nazi crimes.

objectives, although it does not entirely destroy any just component the war otherwise comprised. If it leads, as had been planned by many Allied statesmen, to the destruction of the national existence of a state, the enslaving of its male population, and similar measures, the conditions of peace become every bit as unjust as the war itself. Therefore we repeat: the first factor, the initial just cause, is absolute; the second and the third (the just conduct of war and the just conclusion, the peace) are relative in any assessment of the justice of war. The *right to war*, the initial just cause, can only exist in one of two cases: in the case of a sovereign nation (or a group of allied sovereign nations) exposed to an external threat to their sovereignty and in the case of a nation that has been dispossessed of its once-recognized sovereignty. From this it follows that we are not going to analyze the case of a civil war. In civil wars, as a rule, the citizens of one and the same country fight each other, and the problem on the agenda to be settled with violent means is the change of a social system, not the defense or conquest of national sovereignty.

There are four cases in which such a right to war exists and makes the war *absolutely just* (just without qualification), and two further cases in which an existing right to war makes it only *conditionally just* (subject to certain qualifications). First, the right to war is absolute, the war is absolutely just, when a sovereign nation sees its sovereignty (which is the life and freedom of a sovereign nation and the freedom of its citizens in one, though fundamental, respect) threatened by an enemy. The right is even more emphatic when the nation sees not only the freedom of its citizens (as members of the national body politic whose sovereignty, that is, collective life and freedom, is at stake) but their lives threatened as well by a potentially or actually genocidal enemy. Second, the right to war is absolute, the war is absolutely just, when a once-sovereign state had been dispossessed of its sovereignty (its life and freedom as a body politic, its freedom, as far as its citizens are concerned) under duress. This is an important qualification in an age when politicians and ideologues are ready to declare economic blackmail a sufficient cause of war. Therefore we wish to make it clear that here and in what follows, we mean by "under duress" a situation in which the sovereignty of a nation is threatened, actually or potentially, by an external force threatening the lives and freedom of its citizens.*

---

*We are not discussing here one epistemological problem: whether or not a threat (to life and freedom of the nation, to the freedom, perhaps to the lives, of its

In the first and second case, the right to war remains absolute, the war absolutely just, even if the party exposed to such a threat or dispossessed of its sovereignty starts the war, for in such cases even the offensive is defensive. Third, the right to war exists, the war is absolutely just, in the case of a nation that has been attacked without preliminary warning even if it cannot clearly decide in the confusion thus created whether or not the threat is of such magnitude as to challenge its life and freedom as a nation, and the freedom of its citizens as members of this nation. The only exceptions to this case are case one or case two in which, as mentioned, the triggering of war by the party whose sovereignty is threatened or already dispossessed remains defensive, even if the events start with an attack without warning. Fourth, the right to war exists, and the war is absolutely just, on the part of a nation that accepts it or even formally starts it if it is in alliance with another nation that is waging a just war, as long as the alliance is valid. Here again, seemingly offensive action is in fact defensive action. The declaration of war by the United Kingdom against Germany because of the invasion of Poland was a just and defensive action.

These are the cases, and to our mind the only cases, in which the right to war can be said to be absolute and the war absolutely just. However, one further qualificatory remark is needed. "Being absolutely just" does not alter the proviso that a nation is *not* obliged by any moral maxim to commit itself to war. We emphasize our initial claim that waging a just war is permissible but not morally obligatory. Needless to say, abstention from action because of pragmatic considerations, permissible as it may be, can have tremendous moral and practical consequences: regularly leaving allies to their fate serves to isolate the nation unreliable in its commitments and encourages the aggressor. Nonetheless, abstention is morally permissible. When, however, the right to war is absolutely just, all exhortations addressed to a nation ("to consider higher than its own interests") are to be

---

citizens) is genuine, or mistakenly assessed by the representatives of a people on whom it is incumbent to make a swift decision. Such a mistake can be involuntary or deliberate. But this is a risk that is inherent in every human decision. In the case of wars, of course, the consequences are incomparably more devastating; therefore there is justice in peoples' wrath (and criminal servility in the absence of such wrath) against statesmen who commit such deliberate or involuntary errors of judgment.

rejected as either hypocrisy or cowardice, or advocacy—witting or unwitting—of the aggressor's interests.

The right to war exists, and a war can be said to be just, subject to certain conditions, in two further cases. First, a war is defensible when it is waged, even in the form of an offensive action, against a genocidal regime. Here two qualifications are necessary. The tyrannical, despotic, dictatorial character of a regime does not suffice to justify any external action that may be taken against it; however lightly the word "genocide" is used these days, this and no other condition makes action acceptable. However, if any goal other than the rescue of a whole cluster of people exposed to genocide is being pursued at the conclusion of war, it no longer fulfills the requirement and ceases to be a just war. (This is why Vietnam's rescue operation in Kampuchea cannot ultimately be defended as a just war; it ended with the loss of Kampuchean sovereignty and the installation of a puppet government.) In the present era, which is characterized by an unsavory proliferation of armed liberators, this is a condition that ought to be heeded with particular rigor.

The second case in which the right to war exists, where a war is just but only conditionally, is the one in which a state, earlier dispossessed under duress of crucial parts of its territory vital for its national existence, starts or participates in a war against the former aggressor, alone or in alliance with, or with reliance on, another power. Here two qualifications are necessary: the war cannot be conducted for any objective other than the rectification of the earlier injustice, and any ally cannot itself be engaging in an unjust war. The latter condition was absent in the cases of Hungary and Finland in 1941. After being defeated a year earlier by an overwhelming Soviet power, and veritably under duress, Finland had been forced to relinquish part of its territory. Its full sovereignty had indeed been violated, its existence as a nation had been openly threatened during the war (in the form of the resuscitation of the Karelo-Finn Soviet Republic into which earlier Finland was to be included, an operation in which the "moderate" Andropov commenced his political career), and similar dangers were reasonably expected in the future. Yet despite this, Finland's participation in *Hitler's* war could in no sense be justified. The case of Hungary is similar, though there even the initial motives were incomparably weaker. When a war is only relatively just, it is not only permissible but indeed obligatory for a nation to consider questions other than its sovereignty (its life and freedom as a nation); it must consider such questions as, for

instance, the life and freedom of millions, the targets of one's potentially or actually genocidal ally. In such cases, external warnings to heed
other, ''higher'' considerations do not necessarily lend support to the
interests of an aggressor. (The warning of the United States to Finland
against participating in the German war was one such totally legitimate
warning.)

An analysis of the just or unjust character of war starting from the
second factor, the conduct of war, must take the following factors into
consideration. Above all, valid international treaties, agreements, and
conventions concerning the principles of warfare must, under all conditions, be honored and observed. The execution in the Nuremberg
process of field marshalls Keitel and Jodl was even formally legal, for
they had cosigned, with Hitler (or were in their official capacity responsible for issuing administrative decrees tantamount to such a signature)
orders that legitimized Wehrmacht and SS commanders to commit
murders of prisoners of war on the Eastern front and elsewhere. The
same applied to a number of executed or imprisoned Japanese field
commanders. This is so because, in marked contrast to partisan armies,
both German and Japanese supreme commands had the opportunity to
keep prisoners under at least tolerable conditions. And if not formal
law then certainly natural law demands that this principle should cover
the bestial deeds committed against Soviet prisoners, who had not been
protected by their own government when it refused to sign the Geneva
convention.

However, the number of such valid international agreements is not
excessive; nor are they likely to mushroom in a divided world. Therefore the overarching general principle concerning the just conduct of
war, with certain necessary modifications, again comes from Grotius.
He put it bluntly: War should be conducted against soldiers, not against
women and children. To mention ''necessary modifications'' means
that we are required to address the extremely sensitive issue of the
''terror bombardments'' by Allied powers during World War Two.
Grotius' qualification could have been (but of course was not) honored
in centuries when armies were small, when war was totally separated
from the populations (the majority of which often did not understand
who was who in a particular conflict), and when the production of the
means of warfare took place within a few workshops easily separable
from the general process of production in a given country. Modern
warfare, however, is increasingly *total*. (It was, for instance, in Germany even in the First World War; it was, in all countries, in the Second

World War, and it has remained total in almost all major conflicts in the postwar period.) In a total war, the fabrication of the gigantic modern means of warfare is based on the whole of industry; no part of the economy can be entirely exempted from being part of the war effort. Further, in a total war not only is there a draft, but considerable parts of the older male and the young and old female population work directly in military enterprises for the war. Third, total war is ideological because the active ideological and spiritual support lent to a government (or the withdrawal of such support) by a population is central to the war effort. This results in the tragic fact that war cannot simply be fought against men in uniform, and therefore that it is legitimate, albeit not without qualifications, to extend it to parts of the civilian population.

What kind of qualifications can be introduced here? The conduct of war is just if the armaments industry, raw material sources (oil wells and the like), and all branches of the economy that are vital to the continuation of a war are destroyed in a country that wages an unjust war. The only exception to this would be the use of such means (chemicals) that destroy the general preconditions of civilian life (agricultural production, fresh water supplies, etc.) quite apart from the loss in human life that such means might entail. The destruction of whole German industrial cities or that of Ploesti, the heart of Rumanian oil resources on which Hitler's *Panzerarmee* depended, shows that this is a savage measure but one that should first be considered by those who start unjust total wars. No unequivocal principle can be asserted here, and therefore when we consider the bombardment of cities and other populated areas not primarily because of the industrial targets located in them but to weaken the population's will to continue the war, such military action can be said to be either just though cruel or simply cruel and unjust. In principle, it can be accepted that most—not all—means that accelerate the conclusion of a just war are just, and this can be one of them. Further, such bombardments are meant to protect the lives of those waging a just war, "our" soldiers, and this makes them a just act. (It was thus utterly barbarous of Stalin to become irrationally philanthropic in the major battle for Budapest and limit the amount and scope of his heavy artillery used on the city. As a result of this "magnanimity," tens of thousands of young Russians and Ukrainians fell unnecessarily around and in the city.) On the other hand, there quite clearly are magnitudinal limits to such actions that are difficult, if not outright impossible, to define in advance or to define in technical terms, but beyond which a relatively just act is transformed into an act of barbarism. Here two examples stand out: the destruction of Dresden and, above all, Hiroshima.* However, if people affected by these barbarous acts, citizens or subjects of a nation that waged an unjust war with apparent popular consensus, raise their legitimate grievances, they have to consider another issue in order not to become utterly hypocritical: the absence of revolts and revolutions against their own government, the vocal and tacit support lent by them to the worst imaginable crimes. And the two acts very rarely occur simultaneously.

There is one particular method of conducting war that is irredeemably unjust, even barbarous: violent acts against a populace under permanent or temporary occupation (deportations, terrorizing the inhabitants, looting houses, raping women, and above all, indiscriminately killing unarmed and unprotected people). Acts of this kind can never be justified. Moreover, if they are carried out systematically, on a large scale, and as part of a premeditated plan—these qualifications are crucial—in themselves they would serve to invalidate each and every initially just cause.

While the European continent has seen many wars and very few just peace settlements, in principle it is easy to formulate what the third element of a just war, namely, a just peace, means. Peace is just if the initial cause was just, if the conduct of war has not transformed the just cause into an entirely unjust one, and if the instrument peace agreement, the treaty, aims at nothing other than the objectives already contained in the initial, just cause. Such objectives can be the defense or reconquest of one's sovereignty, the support lent to others to achieve the same goals, or the elimination of a genocidal (but not simply tyrannical, despotic, dictatorial) regime. All peace treaties that go beyond these objectives, either overtly in pursuit of world domination or (as with Wilson) in the form of liberally and sentimentally conceived plans of "global redemption" which in the end serve the greed and the hurt pride of the victors, contaminate the initially just cause to different

---

*The horrific reality of our subject matter is such that one can argue legitimately the other way round. The mass bombardment of Japanese cities (bombing Tokyo with napalm claimed, to our knowledge, more victims than Hiroshima) was still a military necessity when Hiroshima happened. The Japanese resistance, military and civilian, was not yet broken. The occupation of the main island would have cost several hundred thousand, in certain estimates a million, American lives and an inestimable number of Japanese lives. The American soldiers too were human beings; in addition, they did not start a war against Japan. Whereas what can be said in defense of Dresden? When it happened, Germany was already agonizing as a military power. The horrendous destruction of the city was just a cowardly act of revenge.

degrees, depending on the extent of the transgression of the original objectives. Our formulation here is deliberately cautious. No objective observer can deny that Stalin's war against Hitler went far beyond the original, just objectives of an attacked nation; that the outcome of the peace agreement (where one was concluded at all) is not a region of free nations but a new empire. These are serious arguments that mitigate the justice of Russia's war. Those rescued, however, cannot argue without the grave offense of ingratitude against their rescuer, whatever the latter's intentions and later deeds. Nor can one deny, whatever came afterward, that the first priority then was the elimination of Hitler. This simply means that each and every peace settlement extending beyond the just initial cause is unjust (and sows the seeds of future wars), but that there are degrees of justice and injustice to be considered.

Nuclear war transforms the whole problem of just and unjust war (although it does not eliminate the importance of the distinction) in that the new, monstrous means of warfare make the just conduct of war, as well as a just peace settlement, theoretically impossible. As far as the first factor is concerned, the earlier mentioned problem of the magnitude of destruction here attains new dimensions and provides certain paradoxes. For it is far from being evident morally why the destruction of many is "naturally" worse than the destruction of one.* There can be a strictly moralistic argument, as seen above, in terms of which the killing of one is an absolute offense, and therefore the killing of many cannot be "more absolute" (the term is self-contradictory). In this century, there is no absolute argument against an absolutist way of thinking. The following arguments can still be used, however, against the idea of the just conduct of war with nuclear weapons, all based on or related to the magnitude of destruction. First, while it is not a certainty, it is a distinct possibility that nuclear war will result in the end of the whole of humankind. Killing humanity means killing justice as well (where one of the tragic paradoxes of the situation is that killing justice, as we shall see, could be the last act of justice). Second, we have distinguished the destruction of industrial centers, energy resources,

---

*For instance, there is a religious, by definition moral, argument against the *quantitative* view of destroying human lives and related issues. In the aforementioned debate of the dignitaries of the Church of England, P. H. Rippon asked the following question, very consistently on the part of a Christian: "The human body is the temple of the Holy Spirit, wrote St. Paul. Every corpse is an offense against God the Holy Spirit, the giver of life . . . do numbers affect theology? Does it matter less to our Heavenly Father if I kill, not 5,000 but 500 or 5 of his children?" *The Church and the Bomb*, p. 248.

and the like from the destruction of cities with a populace consenting to and supporting an unjust war. We deemed the first just, the second only conditionally so, and even then, only to a degree. A discrimination like this cannot be performed in the case of nuclear weapons; therefore, killing with them is in principle indiscriminate. Third, while the above was a "weak" argument, what follows is absolute. People can be made at least coresponsible for their own tragic fate if they are asked why they did not revolt against it. Such a question cannot be addressed to a future generation that either will be killed by nuclear weapons (if the whole of humankind is exterminated) or, if not, will in all probability be seriously damaged genetically. This would be a generation of totally innocent persons. Another absolute argument against the just conduct of nuclear war is the fate of the noncombatants who inevitably become involved in a war of which neutral states wanted no part. We agree with William C. Gay, who states: "Nuclear war is grossly inefficient with respect to the prospect of sparing noncombatants and, in countervalue strategies, specifically aims at noncombatants."* Finally, it can be theoretically inconsistent but it is certainly humanitarian to argue, when speaking of mass killings, better few than many. This position perhaps does not have weighty arguments behind it, but it is certainly backed by an emphatic feeling which is part of our make-up as long as we are not a Schicklgruber or a Dshugashvili. And from all that has been stated of the impossibility of the just conduct of a nuclear war follows the impossibility of a just (as well as an unjust) peace in conclusion.

The main contradiction buried within our deeply contaminated civilization, however, is that there can be such vital and imperative arguments on behalf of a just cause under threat that make the *conditional* use of nuclear weapons *conditionally just*. (At this point, the great tension between the one absolute and the two conditional components of our theory, a tension caused by a novel and monstrous means of warfare, becomes particularly manifest.) It would be immoral here to argue on the basis of pragmatic considerations. Whichever direction antinuclear theorists and propagandists shift the bulk of responsibility, they will find justifications for the limited use of nuclear weapons on both sides. Nonetheless, the pragmatic argument can be used for one reason. However much we know that both sides lie, and each has pondered the first use of nuclear weapons to destroy the other complete-

*William C. Gay, "Myths about Nuclear War: Misconceptions in Public Beliefs and Governmental Plans," *Philosophy and Social Criticism* (Boston), 9, 2 (1983), p. 134.

ly, the fact that this cannot be included in public argument shows that there is consensus the world over at least concerning one point: the *first all-out use of nuclear weapons with the goal of destroying another social system or a competitor is absolutely unjust, even criminal,* whatever "emancipatory" considerations might lie behind such a decision. The conditional use of nuclear weapons demands, however, different considerations.

The conditional use of nuclear weapons can be conceived of in two distinct scenarios. One is the situation in which a country sees itself exposed to an overwhelming and seemingly unstoppable conventional attack on the part of an enemy the war objectives of which it defines, on the basis of historical evidence, as the destruction of its life and freedom as a nation and the destruction of the freedom of all, the lives of whole clusters, of its citizens. The country in question is convinced that it cannot defend itself in any other way but by using nuclear weapons against the attackers. Given the dimension of such a decision, it must be supported by a preceding or simultaneous almost total consensus. (It is not our concern here to discuss whether the latter is technically feasible.) The second scenario is the use of nuclear weapons by a country that has already suffered a devastating nuclear strike at the hands of an enemy and where the action is no longer a means of defense or victory, but an act of retaliation. Incomparably more people would accept the conditionally just character of the use of nuclear weapons in the first than in the second scenario. In fact, the theoretical place of nuclear weapons in the hypothetical first scenario is what we call deterrent. The deterrent, which is a regulative institution and not a weapon to be used (although its paradoxical nature is such that it is only a valid institution as long as there is the determination eventually to use it), consists of three widely accepted considerations. The first is that we will only use it, and then we would *certainly* use it, if an enemy, whose objectives are such as we have described above, attacks us with overwhelming conventional forces against which we have no other remedy. The second is that we do not start an all-out nuclear war (or a preemptive strike) under any conditions. The third is that, on the basis of our historical experiences, we define our enemy and its objectives as we have above, so that the consequences of subjugation would be murderous for our life and freedom as a member of a body politic and as an individual. There must be a wide consensus concerning all three points. Neither more nor less will suffice for the purposes of a deterrent. If a cluster of people believes that they are entitled, for any substantive considerations whatsoever, to launch a preemptive strike, then the weapon is more than a deterrent and will push the world toward an actual apocalypse. If, on the other hand, people are not ready to use the weapon under any conditions, for different reasons, or if they do not define their enemy as threatening to their individual or collective lives, then the nuclear weapon will not deter anyone from launching an attack if such an attack seems to serve the purposes of an aggressor. Under the conditions of the second scenario, however, many people will say that such an act is superfluous or irrational, in that sense inhumane or an act of revenge. Several extremists among the anti-nuclear theorists will call it a crime against humanity. We would, above all, argue that the blame for such crimes rests with the party that undertook a preemptive strike. Further, we believe that while it is a questionable act (for theoretically it can be the last deed of humankind), it is not immoral; moreover, it is an act of justice, precisely as a retaliation for the terrible crime of a preemptive strike. It is in fact the first theoretical realization of a principle of justice that was first encapsulated in the Roman maxim *Fiat justitia, pereat mundus* (Let there be justice, perish the world), and which has been reaffirmed many times since then by great advocates of justice. Let us avoid misunderstandings: if the aim is the perishing of the world, the act cannot be one of justice; but if the actor refuses to be deterred from his maxim by reference to the collective perishment, it could be.

Even if just and not at all immoral or criminal, however, this is a horrific perspective. Precisely because of this, the permissible and not mandatory character of waging just (in the given case, only conditionally just) wars here prevails powerfully. Pragmatic as well as merciful considerations can deter us from using the deterrent in either a last or a penultimate act of justice. The deterrent is indeed ambiguous: it exists to prevent us from such a situation and it can be the terrible executor of the logic of this very situation. Those who believe, however, that sacrificing our life and freedom as nations and bodies politic, our freedom and huge numbers of our lives as individuals, are not questions of moral consequence make a dreadful mistake themselves, for at least two reasons. First, whatever the "practical merits" of the formula "better Red than dead," it is not a moral maxim, but a maxim of the total rejection of morality. Second, the very act of raising the question of "Shall we renounce our creed, our habits, our institutions, our gods in order to survive?" is in itself the sign of the evaporating of self-confidence, *élan vital*, from a culture, the proof of its inner crisis. Harping on it incessantly pushes the culture even further into the throes of the crisis. And while no one has the right to recommend suicide to others, there is moral truth and judgment in our collective memory, which has preserved with respect the fate of those who had sacrificed their lives rather than seeing themselves bereft of the meaning of life (the Jews of Masada, Indian tribes, Christians besieged by Moslems, Moslems besieged by Christians, Pravoslav believers of the old rite, and several others).

There is a widespread and extremely inaccurate identification of pacifist with antinuclear positions. While it is obvious that all pacifists have to be, by definition, antinuclear, the same is not true in reverse. There are indeed two types of antinuclear militants who are not pacifists: the nationalists, those who supported Thatcher's Falkland war (or at least who were conspicuous in their silence on the issue) despite their otherwise unilateralist position, and the revolutionaries (for whom the "just wars of oppressed people" are commendable acts). Our concern here is with the pacifist who, in modern times, no longer represents a homogeneous, unified type either. The initial hopes of pacifism in the early Enlightenment, the promise that rationalism, liberalism, and industry, individually or conjointly, would bring "eternal peace," are now obviously dead. Pacifism has become either much more resigned or much more radical. The skeptical, resigned type of pacifist is clearly represented by Bertrand Russell, the author of the ominous formula "better Red than dead," which is clearly a partisanship for the universal value of life as against the universal value of freedom (for it is self-evident here that "Red" means "unfree," otherwise the dilemma would be nonexistent). The background of this very doubtful wisdom is excessive skepticism. One cannot know, the skeptic suggests, what is free, what freedom is worth, nor what the value of moral precepts suggested by various prophets is. But one can at least know with certainty where life ends, where death starts. As long as there is life, efforts to regain freedom can be resumed. With more or less consistency, Bertrand Russell maintained this position throughout his career, with one remarkable exception which now, typically, disappears from the antinuclear annals and which is succinctly summed up by I. L. Horowitz: "[in 1945-1951] Russell accepted at face value the Churchillian thesis that only America could save the British Empire. It was during this period that he posed the alternative: either we destroy the socialist spectre, or find the system of benevolent capitalism destroyed."* A different, radical type of pacifist (in whose assessment our position diverges from that of Horowitz) is represented by Lessing,

*Irving Louis Horowitz, *War and Peace in Contemporary Social and Philosophical Theory*, 2nd ed. (London: Condor, 1973), p. 103.

Tolstoy, and Gandhi: they are the men of the Great Refusal. Despite legends, their position is not the sacrifice of the value of freedom on behalf of life. Their conception of pacifism (shared in common without philological interconnections) is summed up by Lessing: peaceful disobedience to oppressive powers voids them of their oppressive force. Power is not a mythical entity. *We are power*, our submission to and collaboration with tyrants and oppressors. Without our submission there is no tyranny. Therefore, the habitual "revolutionary" criticism of this type of pacifism (for instance, Lenin's critique of Tolstoy) was doubly wrong. First, it dismissed with contempt the "childish" assumption that world-correcting violence could bring more evil in the world than could already be found in it anyhow, a thesis which was powerfully corroborated by Lenin himself and even more by his successors. Second, and equally important, the "revolutionary" critique pretended that the "men of the Great Refusal" wished to sacrifice freedom (social transformation, emancipation) on the altar of the sanctity of life.

In fact, Lessing, Tolstoy, and Gandhi demanded not "less than necessary" active effort but "more than humanly possible." When Gandhi decided against an anti-Hitler war, he was no forerunner of present-day self-Vichyization (which is, for reasons which we will see, a better term than "Finlandization"), for the decision was moral, not "zoological" (it did not aim at the mere survival of the species). What Gandhi preached, but what was apparently beyond general, human endurability, was a nonviolent, nonetheless total disobedience to tyrannical powers, which would thus bring the latter to a complete halt. In a way, this apparently infantile idea contains a deep wisdom. Thus Hannah Arendt argued brilliantly that all-embracing political revolutions more often than not happen peacefully, when general disobedience paralyzes the machinery of oppression, when the transformation is nonviolent because the agencies of coercion no longer obey commands.* Nor can it be denied in principle that the peaceful and collective acts of Great Refusal can lead in the future to further revolutions. This model cannot, however, serve the purposes of Western antinuclear movements and trends, for it is suited only to conditions of political tyranny.

*Hannah Arendt, *On Revolution* (New York: Viking, 1976), pp. 263–70. Following her analysis, we began to understand the Hungarian Revolution of 1956 as precisely one such gigantic act of Great Refusal. Abominable as the outcome is, the way the antishah revolution gained victory in Iran was exactly the same.

"Life or liberty"—this alternative, which almost inevitably crops up in the writings, posters, slogans, and discussions of the antinuclear movement, has been described by us as a symptom of crisis, an antinomy, neither pole of which can or should be chosen against the other. The message of our present analysis is that the Left (contingents of which are part of the antinuclear movement but not coextensive with it) must not choose between the thesis and antithesis of the antinomy: all such choices would mean a theoretical and practical self-mutilation. The unity of freedom and life as universal values, as common measures of the level of humanity of our civilization, must be maintained, or else the democratic Left would have resigned its historical mission. Nor is it a practical necessity to accept such a self-mutilating choice. The duty of social movements that are aware of the present dangers but want to transform the present constellation is precisely to reformulate the problems by practically creating a new social field of alternatives. This, not the mystic-heroic acceptance of collective death, the suicide of our civilization, nor the internalization of slavery, is the road toward life and liberty.

# II.    Are We Closer to a Nuclear World War?

Implicitly or explicitly, the pathos of the antinuclear movement originates from the emphatic affirmative answer its advocates give to the question in the title of this chapter. Let us quote in a random way from a pamphlet, originating in West Germany in a Green-dominated atmosphere but quite characteristic of the whole West European antinuclear movement, entitled *Initiative for an East-West Dialogue*: "We Europeans have all become hostages of the superpowers. We can instantly be annihilated by a decision from above. It appears as if we are living in civilian societies. *In reality, we are in a pre-war state.*"

Our book is written with the intention of providing a direct refutation of this atmosphere of an impending nuclear holocaust, as well as against the accompanying self-dramatization and conspiracy theories that abound. It is our firm conviction that we are not a step nearer to a global nuclear war than we have been for decades; that no technological factors, no new families of modern weapons can serve as proof of an impending nuclear world war; that no social theory, unless it succumbs to an extreme fetishism, should explain the danger and immediacy of a world war through technological factors alone; that no social analysis can authenticate the assumption that the dominant and obviously conflicting trends in world politics are at a point of no return, on the part of either the American or the Soviet leadership. It is our equally firm conviction that widely held fears and views of this kind do not crop up by mistake or "accidentally." There are powerful tensions in the present Western constellation that are acted out in the form of the fear of nuclear holocaust. For these tensions to be analyzed, one theoretically has to eliminate from the discourse the imagery (not the arguments, which unfortunately do not abound in the antinuclear manifestos) of an impending nuclear doomsday.

As far as we can see, there are four social preconditions whose existence would make a nuclear world war a possibility, even a probability. Two of these factors would suffice on their own for such a probability, but two of them are only sufficient together with the rest. A global nuclear war would be possible, even probable, first, if either of the superpowers believed in the possibility that it (but not its enemy) could survive such a war, even if with heavy casualties; and second, if one or, even more, both were entangled in a crisis of a kind from which any nonmilitary outlets would be discarded by the leading strata of the superpowers (in the case of Western societies, by considerable sections of public opinion as well). But even if the second precondition were to exist, it would mean an imminent danger of global nuclear war only if the first (the belief in survival) were also the case. Third, such a world war would be possible, even probable, if the leading strata of the United States believed in the survivability of such a war (the first precondition), if they had an image of the future that would promise a return to a pre–World War Two, preferably pre-1917, stage of world affairs, and if American society were militarized to a sufficient degree to mobilize the majority in support of, and to suppress any opposition to, such a strategy.* Finally, such a war would be possible, even probable, if either of the superpowers pursued a policy that would threaten the other at one of its vital lifelines with (and perhaps in a moment of gripping hysteria, even without, unlikely as it is) the belief in survivability after an all-out nuclear war. If the first condition were the case, those who happened to survive would already be beyond the nuclear holocaust. If the first were not the case, but either the second or the fourth were, we would have, indeed, made a gigantic step toward nuclear World War Three, and the pathos of the antinuclear movement would be largely justified. The same applies if the third were the case.

In this chapter we will mainly analyze the presence or absence of these preconditions on the part of the United States, leaving discussion of the Soviet dynamic and strategy to chapter 3. This is all the more justified as even in the nonunilateralist sections of the antinuclear movement (and not necessarily among its Leftist contingents) the view

---

*At this point, we mention a precondition applicable to one of the superpowers only. The reason is that we believe that the Soviet Union, or more precisely its ruling oligarchy, does have an image of the future from which the enemy is eliminated, and we are also convinced that efficient opposition to such a policy is paralyzed.

has emerged, for several historical reasons, that the United States alone is responsible for the present tensions or that the United States is actively preparing to fight a nuclear war in the near future. If, in analyzing the first necessary precondition of an impending or rapidly approaching nuclear world war, we depart from the visible parts of the military doctrines of *both* superpowers, we could easily come to the frightening conclusion that both of them indeed believe that the ''better prepared'' could survive a nuclear world war and that, therefore, under certain circumstances it may be a feasible venture. Pentagon officials have confirmed several times either their belief in the winnability of such a war or the existence of strategic documents containing such beliefs. Very much in contrast to the antinuclear propaganda, Soviet military doctrine, as confirmed in almost all official speeches of all Soviet ministers of defense since Malinowski, has always contained the idea that the nuclear war, albeit ''horrible,'' can be won.* This is, of course, perfectly ''natural'' in the sense that military bureaucracies must somehow legitimize their self-perpetuation, prerogatives, ever increasing share of budgetary allocations, and hermetic-secretive separation from the rest of the world. At the same time this, and not any science fiction ideas about an ''accidental world war,'' is the really menacing factor. However, we shall immediately see that the situation is not so unequivocal in the case of military bureaucracies either. As far as the United States is concerned, the frequent refraining from the use of nuclear weapons in situations where military considerations would have otherwise dictated their use† can be explained by the pressure of internal and worldwide public opinion, perhaps much more than by the leadership's own abhorrence of nuclear weapons. But what of the Soviet Union, where there is no inner public opinion whatsoever and which has never cared (from Hungary, 1956, to Poland, 1981) about the

---

*In an article we have quoted H. Hoffmann, the minister of defense of the GDR who expressly rebukes ''benevolent pacifists'' for the misbelief that thermonuclear war cannot be part of a socialist strategy; it is and would be the ''continuation of class struggle with different means,'' which is indeed the Soviet view. See F. Fehér and A. Heller, ''On Being Anti-Nuclear in Soviet Societies,'' *Telos* 57 (Fall 1983), pp. 144–62. The reference made there is to Heinz Hoffmann, *Aus Reden und Aufsätzen*, 1974 bis Juni 1978, Berlin (Ost), 1979, p. 221.

†It is a documented fact that Douglas MacArthur wanted to use nuclear weapons against the superior numbers of the Chinese in the Korean War. Richard Nixon, early in his career, suggested the use of nuclear bombs in the war in Indochina, and William Westmoreland, who had constantly considered, but for the possible Chinese intervention, a direct attack on Hanoi, could have been offered the ''nuclear guarantee'' and yet was not. There must be several other moments of consideration of which we are unaware.

international echo of its acts? In our view, the only explanation is that despite public statements, which are designed to legitimize the existence and growth of military bureaucracies, *none of the leading strata of the superpowers believes in the winnability of nuclear war, or in the possibility of surviving it.* Adamant as we are as far as the existence of Soviet expansionism is concerned, we do not believe for a moment that the Soviet Union, which is at least abreast if not ahead of the West (once again, we are no judges of this military problem), is actually preparing to wage an all-out nuclear war now, in the near future, or at any time. Its experts must possess frightening technical information concerning the striking capacity of the other side as well as the aftermath of such a war.

The assertion that the governments of the superpowers do not believe in the survivability of an all-out nuclear war needs further clarification in light of the article by William Gay mentioned previously. He speaks there of a *distorted communication* both in "public myths" (the myths of antinuclear movements) and on the part of governmental agencies (p. 137), the roots of which he believes can be found in the dynamics of "commodity fetishism." While this explanation seems to be too abstract for us, we asserted at the beginning a similar conviction: the antinuclear syndrome should be understood from its social context, and not the other way round.

It is Gay's express and well-founded view that the two cardinal articles of faith in public antinuclear myths, namely, unsurvivability and unrecoverability in the wake of a nuclear war, are indeed myths. "My point is here," he states, "that recovery potential in at least some places on the planet, even if very slow in significant actualization, is likely" (p. 126). More specifically, he adds, the public myth generally totally misunderstands the concept "overkill."

> MAD (mutual assured destruction) is not equivalent to "biocide." . . . The notion of "assured destruction" was developed in the early 1960s by then Secretary of Defense, Robert S. McNamara. He argued that the potential of the U.S. to destroy 20–25% of the Soviet population and over 50% of Soviet industry would be a sufficient deterrence against any Soviet attack. . . . The meaning of "overkill," then, is not senseless stockpiling of nuclear weapons beyond a level sufficient to achieve biocide. Rather, "overkill" refers to nuclear capacity beyond the (varying) requirements for "assured destruction"; specifically, it is linked to potential delivery failures. (pp. 129–30)

If this is true, then in what sense is our statement true that the superpower governments do not believe in survivability despite propaganda and strategic jargon to the contrary? It is true in the sense that governments are also aware of the grave facts spelled out in Gay's paper:

> [T]he falsity of the public myths does *not* supply *sufficient* conditions for victory. . . . Beyond survivors and recovery potential, some of the further necessary conditions for victory include preservation of key national institutions and maintenance of political obedience, i.e., the avoidance of anarchy. . . . When "acceptable" death tolls for the victor run from 20 million to 100 million and even more, semantic considerations are no longer irrelevant. . . . When the connotative sense of "victory" is confronted in its broad qualitative dimensions, the sentiment of citizens in the surviving national remnants may well be that the distinction between which side "won" and which side "lost" is trivial. (pp. 134–35).

In much simpler language, the following conclusions can be deduced: (1) A "victorious" state can survive a nuclear war in the sense of biocide (in other words, living human beings will remain after a nuclear war), but it cannot survive *as a nation, as a state*, because its key national institutions will break down and political and civil anarchy will reign supreme, which to all practical purposes spells the death of the state. In this sense, *for the governments, but also for the populace, a nuclear war is not survivable*. (2) As a result of the enormous death toll, the survivors will feel no difference between victory and devastating defeat. Therefore they will positively feel hatred against those who had pushed them into such a situation. In this sense again, for governments and other political agencies a nuclear war, lost or won, suggests little chance of survival. It was this, and not biocide, that we meant when we mentioned that the superpower governments are fully aware that nuclear wars cannot be survived.

For methodological reasons, we proceed here from the third hypothetical precondition: Does the United States have an image of the future that would predict a possible return to the pre-1917 situation (that is, to a world without Soviet Russian and Chinese communism), together with the adequate strategic self-confidence and militarized state of American society mandatory for preparing for an immediate war? Everyone who glances with a minimum of objectivity at American society knows that it is certainly not coextensive with the views reflected in the speeches of President Reagan. In fact, the contrary is the case. Whoever is able to distinguish the clamorous and sometimes bellicose speeches of the president from the actual state of American society will know that America, for reasons to be analyzed later, has never regained its strategic self-confidence after Vietnam. The demand for a ''stronger America'' (which swept Reagan to power in 1980) was a direct reply to the weakness of the American stance in—to mention only one example—Iran, where the American leadership, very much in contrast to Soviet resoluteness in Poland, did not use the Iranian military contingents to suppress a fomenting revolution and suffered a devastating political defeat as a result. It is generally acknowledged that this weakness has not subsided, as could be seen throughout the crisis in Poland, notwithstanding some ludicrous media gestures and largely ineffective embargos. Even Soviet vulnerability in the war in Afghanistan is very far from being fully exploited by the United States, clearly in fear of possible Soviet incursions into Pakistan, which the Americans, unlike at the time of Korea, are no longer prepared to contain. Afghan guerrillas certainly live on American military aid, otherwise obviously they could not have been able to fight for four years, but the military build-up simply cannot be compared with that lent by the Soviet Union to North Vietnam and its southern guerrilla fighters. As far as the militarization of American society is concerned, what any unbiased observer can report is the exact contrary of a militarized society. With all the jingoism around (to which the wide success of such a conservative-patriotic movie as *The Deerhunter* testifies), the first signal of a possible restoration of the draft provoked such a wholesale propaganda of defeatism that it gave birth to the new historic slogan of what we have called self-Vichyization: ''Nothing is worth dying for.'' Whereas sections of public opinion demand the fortification of the United States as a superpower, there are unmistakable signs of discontent whenever it costs American lives, a sacrifice which is inevitable for a hegemonic power and which had been endured tight-lipped, even with pride, in the heyday of British colonial might. Apart from the fact that equally important sections of American public opinion try to curb American aggressiveness in the only region where it is fully manifest, Central America, there is another factor that American policy makers must confront: the increasing suspicion about, sometimes outright contempt for, American military valor. This contempt was clearly expressed in an interview with A. Urban by Halsti, the Finn general and historian, veteran of Finland's war against the Soviet Union and later its war against Germany, a skeptical realist and partisan of Finland's subservience to the Soviet Union. What can the world expect from an army, he asked rhetorically, whose soldiers shot in great numbers their commanding officers, rebelled and disobeyed in the Vietnam War, and got away with it, with at best a symbolic punishment? All these facts could be interpreted in several different ways according to one's national affiliation, political commitment, and value preferences, but we hardly believe that the facts themselves can be denied. If this is so, the strategic self-confidence necessary for any war preparation is totally missing from American society; so is militarism in a socially organized and consensually accepted way.

In fact, the strategy of the United States during the last forty-four years, since America reentered world politics directly after withdrawing in a post–World War One isolationism, has undergone four distinct stages of development. The first spans the period from the beginning of World War Two (Pearl Harbor) to the death of Franklin D. Roosevelt. This was a period of the birth of American strategic self-confidence, characterized by a strange combination of sincere and enthusiastic liberalism and shrewd determination to establish American world hegemony. The first factor inspired an honest and resolute stance against Nazism (Roosevelt was just as dogmatic in this respect as Joseph Stalin, and much more so that Winston Churchill); the second factor inspired bold strategic conceptions looking far beyond immediate victory (in the Pacific, in Asia, almost invariably to the detriment of the British Empire) in pursuit of its own political interests distinct from both of its allies. This strategy contained a number of fatal misconceptions. The most important were the underestimation of the strength of the Soviet Union, deeming Stalin's Russia a junior partner in American world hegemony, and the underrating of the opportunities and strength of Chinese communism while overestimating the inner reserves of Chiang Kai-shek's regime.

The second period, roughly spanning the time from Potsdam to the moment when the Vietnam venture proved to be the first ever American defeat, covers almost a quarter of a century. This was, albeit with weakening pace and vigor, a period of American world hegemony. This was indeed extended to the greater part of the world, and no Western competitor for this hegemony remained. Further, certain hitherto enemy nations were included as allies and economic (occasionally, military) additions to the Western system. The system itself was an American success as well. For a while in this period the hope of a ''roll-back of the Iron Curtain'' was maintained, primarily in Asia and to some extent in Eastern Europe as well, although, as events in Hungary in 1956 showed, in the latter area it was rather a propagandistic exercise.

Near the end of this period, however, the strategic hopes started to wane; the system had gradually eroded.

The third period was short and was characterized by an incomparably more lucid but cynical and skeptical self-consciousness than any period before: this was the Kissinger era, lasting until the middle of the 1970s. Henry Kissinger, the disciple of Metternich, that master diplomat of a declining world power and *jongleur* of survival, took as his point of departure the firm conviction that communist victory, where it had been achieved, is irrevocable, and liberal, or even nonliberal, capitalist rule over the whole of the world is no longer conceivable (at least not in the foreseeable future of present civilization, and a politician must not be a prophet). His was a strategy of retreat and fortification of the remaining positions of the West, with as much Machiavellianism and unscrupulousness as necessary. His was a politics that certainly wanted to maintain American military might (without which a retreat would degenerate into a rout), but that it was a defensive strategy is beyond doubt. Its institutional innovation, sometimes regarded as détente but which was little more than the rationalized managing of a *condominium*—the direct and secret negotiations between the two superpowers, accepting the adequate doctrines concerning the respective spheres of influence (the Brezhnev and Schonfeld doctrines, both important additions to the Yalta-Potsdam complex)—meant a certain amount of stability, with bilateral conservative supremacy in the management of world affairs.

It is precisely this stability that has disappeared in the fourth, the present stage of American history, without any regaining of the strategic self-confidence necessary for an upsurge of expansionism. Its typical hero is President Reagan himself, perhaps the most unpopular of postwar American presidents as far as world public opinion is concerned. His policy substantiates our claim of a lack of strategic self-confidence, even that of a coherent strategic conception in American policy planning. On the one hand, Reagan regularly gives low-level, moralizing, and ideologically bellicose speeches against communism in the worst vocabulary of the cold war period; at the same time, he pushes through a new cycle in nuclear armament updating. The latter can have, and in all probability does have, several functions: giving impetus to the economy in the only way feasible for a period of very low investment (this is the Zaslavsky-Piccone argument); performing a military function mandatory for all administrations that do not accept the idea of an armament freeze, namely, the updating of the American army; and paying lip service to the upsurge of feelings in favor of a "stronger America," which was Reagan's electoral basis in the race against Jimmy Carter. But there is, in all probability, an important additional dimension of this policy that perhaps in the clearest way shows the total absence of any strategic conception, the lack of any feasible image of the future in present-day American policy making. There are good reasons to assume that the present upsurge in rearmament is motivated also by the belief that driving the Soviet leadership into a new cycle in arms development will ruin their country economically. Such an idea has three major flaws. First, we have demonstrated in our book, *Dictatorship Over Needs*, as have several other analysts of the problem, that the Soviet regime is not oriented to profit and economic rationality, and therefore it cannot be financially ruined. The only thing that could eventuate from such a policy is to force the Soviet leadership to employ Stalin's methods of mass terrorizing. Second, a policy of this kind totally ignores the increasing Russian-nationalist component in Soviet life, the only factor which can create a somewhat active consensus around the Soviet leadership. Finally, the whole policy is nothing but a passive expectation of miracles, the exact opposite of the facade created by bellicose speeches, a stance which could never produce strategic yields. In addition, it has been accompanied by the truly dangerous fact that the Reagan administration has almost formally destroyed the channels of confidential communication between the two superpowers. The almost formal breaking of relations with the other nuclear superpower is a sign of imbalance in American policy making, the only one which has created legitimate fears in the eyes of world opinion. For it is bad enough that our world is managed by superpowers, but it is even worse if it is not comanaged at all.

In the foregoing we have already given a refutation, at least as far as the United States is concerned, of the fourth hypothetical precondition of an impending or rapidly approaching nuclear world war. Without strategic self-confidence, or even a clear image of the future, the United States is not endangering any vital life line of the Soviet Union; it does not even exert excessive pressure, such as might be regarded by the Soviets as a *casus belli*, on the Soviet empire. (What we have stated about Poland and Afghanistan applies here.) Nor, similarly, is there any evidence to suggest that the Soviet Union is situated any differently with respect to the fourth precondition, despite its clearly expansionist present tendencies. This is also true regarding Central America, where the American policy makers are, rightly or wrongly, concerned that the regimes in transition tend to become Soviet satellites and, more importantly, Soviet rocket-launching pads. If this were so, it might produce an effect similar to what a vigorous American intrusion into Poland during the Solidarity crisis would have produced (which is an untenable assumption bearing in mind the Western record in Eastern Europe). However, even this would not be tantamount to an impending, let alone inevitable, nuclear world war. In the Middle East, which is for obvious reasons another vital spot for "the West" (Japan included), Soviet expansion, albeit much more vigorous than any American attempts in regions vital for the Soviet Union, is realistic and cautious enough not to provoke a final clash. *Casus belli* is a remarkably meaningful phrase: a war, even one that in its effects cannot be compared to a nuclear holocaust, must have a cause more valid and concrete than the competing character of coexisting world-systems *in abstracto*, and there seems to be no such imminent cause on the horizon. More important evidence concerning the impending (or rapidly nearing) nuclear world war would be the undeniable fact that there are indeed crises of different kinds in both social systems. We have analyzed in our *Dictatorship Over Needs* what kind of crisis the Soviet regime is facing. In *The West and the Left* we commented on the causes, the character, and the possible outcome of the Western crisis. We would not deny, indeed we would wish to emphasize, the largely illusory character of the perspectives of overcoming the respective crises in both societies: in the West, we reject the belief in miraculous and boundlessly elastic possibilities for investment that will ensure the infinite spiral of growth; in the East, we reject the ideology of the Soviet power elite, that expansionism will "export" the inner problems and their solutions will thus produce a conflict-free state of affairs within the Soviet regime proper. Belief in illusory solutions, however, is an important social fact, proof of the existence of, and actions toward the realization of, hopes. Such an atmosphere is certainly not identical with the utter and desolate despair necessary for many millions to plunge themselves in the throes of a nuclear world war.

We therefore cannot see the presence of any of the necessary preconditions that would corroborate the "Sarajevo atmosphere" prevailing in the antinuclear movement. There is sufficient reason to feel indignation at the wasting of human resources and energies on a futile arms race in which there is no victory, no "final stage" for either partner irrespective of whether and for whom it would be good or bad if there were such. There is equally sufficient reason to emphasize the excessive sufferings of important areas of the world caused by either one or both of the superpowers (Eastern Europe, the Middle East, Central

America, and, to some extent, Indochina, although there the responsibility is to a very great extent endogenous). Within the general criticism of American policy there is good reason for emphasizing that breaking off relations between the two superpowers and passively waiting for the collapse of the other under the burden of its inner contradictions is not only ludicrous but to some extent even dangerous. In our firm view, however, there is absolutely no objective reason to feel and behave as if we were on the brink of a global nuclear war.

But are we living in the midst of a new cold war? In terms of the antinuclear catechism this question, too, has to be answered in the affirmative. Nonetheless, we believe such an answer to be entirely false. The general evidence provided by the antinuclear spokespeople concerning the new cold war reduces to one (or all) of the following factors: the bellicose character of the speeches of President Reagan; the new, intensified cycle of rearmament, which is probably taking place with equal speed in the case of both superpowers but which, because of the public character of vital budgetary issues in the United States, is easily demonstrable in one case, not so easily in the other; the highly destructive technological propensities of the new family of missiles (for instance, the extreme speed of the Pershing missile). However, this seems to be an emotional and inconsistent mode of argumentation. These factors, properly inserted into a relevant context, can or cannot establish the danger or even imminence of a nuclear world war, but they do not constitute, either separately or together, an answer to the question of whether we are living in a new cold war.

We believe that the existence of a cold war can be determined according to the following objective criteria. A first requirement is a total (or almost total) (West) European-American unity, presumably under American ''leadership,'' which confronts an equally, although differently, unified East. The conflicts between them must be exclusively East versus West in nature. Second, there must be a concerted preparation, military, political, ideological, and propagandistic, for a confrontation with the communist world, an objective which must be sincerely shared at least by a considerable part of the organizers and supporters of the cold war atmosphere. Third, there must be a total break-off of relations of all kinds between the two worlds, a state of absolute noncommunication. Fourth, the inner opposition to such a concerted Western plan would have to be crushed or, where this is only possible at the cost of sacrificing the liberal-parliamentary regime (as would have been the case of Italy and France during the cold war), restrictive measures and legislation should be introduced against it. Leftists would have to be ousted from all government and other influential and confidential positions; if and where it is possible, they would have to be physically silenced. This is the well-known state of McCarthyism. Finally, historically but perhaps organically, the essence of the cold war was such that while "hot wars" were fought outside Europe (in Asia), the potentially most dangerous East-West tensions were located within Europe.

For logical reasons, we shall commence our analysis with the fifth factor. It seems to corroborate conspicuously the position of those who argue that a new cold war is here. Indeed, Western Europe is once again the center of a major political storm. But it is here that the similarity ends. The present tension is not a primarily East versus West conflict, rather it is a rebellion of "Europe" against American hegemony. It is, therefore, a conflict within the West. As a result, the first and perhaps fundamental condition of a cold war situation is absent at present. There is no longer any Western unity, not even a relative one. The Western alliance, for reasons that historically and politically are well deserved, lives in the throes of a deep crisis. Here, we would only comment on one question that repeatedly reemerges in the antinuclear discourse: the "colonization" of Europe by the present superpowers. Whereas the quest for neutrality is a morally neutral question, a false and misleading moral pathos in the pinnacle of the discourse is not. It is questionable to what extent a subject called "Europe" exists, even more to what extent it had existed before the war. But if it did, it was, together with Japan, the main agent responsible for the outbreak of World War Two. While we would be the last to defend Stalin's Soviet Union (which from the moment of its admission into international power politics, namely, the Molotov-Ribbentropp pact, immediately began its expansionist career), it is hardly deniable that the nucleus of aggression was constituted by the European Fascist and Nazi countries. Equally, it can hardly be denied that France and England first experimented with Hitler as a potential anti-Bolshevik weapon but later could not contain the impetus they had set in motion. In this sense, "Europe" has wasted its role as the "natural," "traditional" center of world politics, and despite European frustration, such a role can hardly be restored.

It must be equally clear to all objective witnesses that none of the second, third, or fourth preconditions of a cold war applies to the present situation. Not only has the critical tone toward the USSR been gradually reduced but, in some countries and in the liberal press, negative views of the Soviet system are simply banned. None other than Mrs. Thatcher spelled out, on the occasion of the invasion of Grenada, that the armed liberation of oppressed nations can lead to "terrible wars" and therefore should not be practiced. The "rolling back" of communism is not even formally part of European conservative policy any longer. There is no need to say much about the third condition: tourist, political, and economic contacts between East and West are booming. As to the fourth condition, the repression of inner opposition, we can only say that there are more socialist governments in Europe today than ever (some of which include the participation of communists), and the streets are dominated by the antinuclear movement.

On the surface the political storm is centered on the concept, institution, and vehicles of the *deterrent*. It rages around the central hypothetical question: in the unlikely case of need, can or cannot the deterrent be used? In other words, what does it mean "to prepare for a nuclear war"? We have argued that a nuclear war cannot be fought except under certain extreme circumstances. This qualification means, first, that the thermonuclear deterrent, while it consists overwhelmingly of weapons of attack, must not be used other than in defense, and even then only in utmost extremity (or in retaliation for a previous preemptive strike). This circumstance, of course, rewrites the whole traditional strategic dichotomy of defense and attack. Further, while the deterrent is a moral institution, it is one with deep contradictions which, as we have argued, are the contradictions of our whole present culture.*

The apocalyptic view of the nuclear holocaust, in its full gloomy

*This statement is not identical with the formulation originally given in the draft of "The Church and the Bomb," which reads as follows: "The ethics of deterrence are the ethics of threatening to do something which one believes to be immoral, which one intends to do only in circumstances which will not arise because of the conditional threat" (p. 241). This is an incorrect formulation, for the following reasons. First, the existence of the deterrent without using it is moral, not immoral, because it prevents atrociously immoral deeds, and ultimately it is the *actual existence, not the hypothetical use*, of the deterrent that is under discussion. Second, the hypothetical use of the deterrent, for all ethics that do not regard God as the sole judge in earthly affairs, and which put on freedom a moral emphasis equal to life, is not immoral, but morally contradictory. It destroys an enormous amount of human lives, among them those of totally innocent people. This is the ineradicably barbarous face of our civilization which we can only deny, with or without deterrent, in utter hypocrisy. At the same time, it constitutes a *punishment* for the attack on our freedom and lives, and in this sense it is, as analyzed, an act of justice, even if "a ruthless act."

majesty, arises precisely against this background and has two distinct functions. It has to fortify the feeling that we are nearing Armageddon, that "the writing is on the wall," and it has to contribute to the dismantling of the deterrent. This is of course not to say that the nuclear holocaust is a marionette play projected on a worldwide screen by shrewd manipulators with a fine sense of melodrama (although there are manipulators galore in the movement, and the sense of melodramatics is indeed let loose). Just the contrary. We are facing a (one hopes short-lived) life feeling of a whole civilization with a double edge. On the one hand, the forecast of the Apocalypse is a legitimate, even extremely important memento of the strategic self-complacency, the "war-game spirit" of bureaucracies which we mentioned above and termed a genuine danger. On the other hand, it is unambiguously the voice of Western self-defeatism.

What kind of images appear in the collective imagination about the nuclear holocaust? Above all, the end of the world, literally a doomsday, a life feeling that invariably appears at the gravest junctures in all civilizations. It is not necessary to go back as far as the Roman world in which, as a response to the crisis of that civilization, Christianity wrote the *memento mori* on the wall. In recent times, European people lived in a very similar atmosphere during and after World War One (which was in fact the collapse of the nineteenth-century world), expressed in the form of both apocalyptic arts and messianic politics. Many believe that we are witnessing the collective suicide of a civilization, the first in written history, a result of the genie released from the bottle, of intemperate industrialization. Anti-industrialist, not anticapitalist, life feeling is the authentic expression of the attitude of the majority in the antinuclear movement. This is an extremely important attitude, one which, if the crisis is overcome, could lead to the positive and absolutely necessary projects of alternative technological developments. However, these feelings of either an end of the world or the first collective suicide of a civilization are typical symptoms of a *practically atheist culture without emancipatory social projects*. The actors understand the technological implications but they are most reluctant to draw moral consequences (other than sporadically fundamentalist ones) concerning the causes of the present constellation. People now live in a community of fear and insecurity in huge numbers. Those manipulating these widespread feelings in good faith (in that they regard it as their moral and prophetic duty to rescue the world) or in bad faith (for party or business motives) perforce intensify fear and insecurity in order to exploit it for their purposes, prophetic or otherwise. This is a radical change when compared with militarist-nationalist and revolutionary traditions, both of which have suggested, even demanded, the ignoring of sacrifices in the name of some higher, overarching community. (Here, and not with satirical purposes, we have to remind the reader of Mao Zedong's extremely optimistic attitude toward a nuclear world war at the world conference of communist parties in Moscow in 1960. It was consistent on his part to disregard the possible death of perhaps 60 percent of humankind.) Without such systematic exploitation of the community of fear and insecurity neither the conviction that World War Three is coming closer day by day nor the suspicion of, or hostility toward, the deterrent can be achieved. (And the sociopsychological "secret" of the deterrent, as another participant in the discussion on "the Church and the Bomb" correctly put it, is that it has to be believed in.) The discourse centered on nuclear holocaust therefore considers survival or collective death as the only questions worthy of consideration. The *meaning* of life is no longer on the agenda.

What, in fact, are we to expect from a nuclear holocaust: "biocide," the extermination of the whole species? Here, even more than with respect to the technological capabilities of modern weapons, obscurity and incertitude prevail. In armament technology, there is at least safe and reliable (because experimentally tested) knowledge, even if it is hidden from the public eye. As far as the aftermath of nuclear war is concerned, knowledge would only come with the test that must not come. Therefore, ideologically motivated forecasts and doomsday fiction abound on an incomparably larger scale than in the pseudomilitary discussion of the antinuclear movement. Those who have advocated a new cold war, and even preemptive nuclear strikes against the enemy, like Edward Teller, use their well-deserved scientific authority irresponsibly in predicting that the USSR will "only" suffer casualties of the magnitude of those during World War Two. Most forecast experts of the antinuclear movement will occasionally present scenarios that predict the total extinction of the whole of humankind. (We have seen the interpretation of "assured destruction" and "overkill" in W. C. Gay's article, an interpretation which we find convincing and which explicitly *denies* the identification of biocide and MAD or overkill.) What we can, more or less safely, assume with certainty is the following. The casualties in a war waged today with modern conventional (nonnuclear) weapons would be incomparably larger, as far as both armies and the civilian populace are concerned, than those of World War Two. (This seems to be convincingly demonstrated by the Vietnam

War.) From this, inferences predicting terrible losses of human life in an all-out nuclear clash can be made but no knowledge of the end of humankind can be achieved. In all probability, the main losers, the absolute victims, would be the cities, the centers of industry, government, and hoarded supplies of food, medicines, fuel. The power and communication system of the modern world would break down, supplies and resources would be widely contaminated; societies would become ungovernable in a modern sense, for all central authorities would disappear. A gigantic new migration of survivors (toward continents and regions unaffected or less destroyed) would commence, with the accompanying barbarization of the more favored communities, which would do everything to protect their limited advantages. In this sense, the "last of the wars" would by no means be the end of wars. New, adverse changes in the face and functioning of nature surrounding the survivors would take place, although there is again no knowledge, just negative myths, to foretell exactly what kind and of what scope these will be. Institutions and stored facilities of accumulated knowledge would be overwhelmingly wiped out, and survivors would lose with them several of humankind's crucial skills and a considerable part of its collective memory. There would be, in all probability, genetic harm done to future generations, although again, there is more hypothesis than knowledge in the predictions. We do not even have an accurate assessment, if such can be made at all, of the genetic damage done in Hiroshima. Surviving humankind would live certainly without the luxury of freedom and, after the Fall, with very little respect for human life. The survivors would not resemble the noble savage, for they would have too much accumulated knowledge on the membranes of their collective memory. Neither would they resemble Promethean man, for the tools required to storm the heavens would be largely destroyed. Therefore, the question is not simply one of Life and Death, the Manichean alternative of antinuclear myths, but the loss of the good life, a certain meaning of life without which we simply cannot live.

The antinuclear movement bases itself on the criticism, and ultimately the rejection, of the deterrent. The rejection can be immediate and unilateral, or its abolition can be assumed as a result of a long process. In Europe, the two main contingents of the movement, the British and the German, represent these two poles: the British the first, the German (to which recently the German Social Democratic party has been added with its antimissile policy) the second, although the

Greens are unilateralist. Their criticism of the deterrent is twofold: moral and practical. Sometimes these criticisms appear together, sometimes individually. In discussing the problematic of the "right to war," we have already set forth our views on the moral questions involved. Here, we add only two further arguments. The first concerns a degree of hypocrisy found in some arguments against a deterrent force. According to this, no nuclear deterrent should be deployed on European soil given the obvious dangers involved in warehousing the weapons. On the other hand, one should not withdraw from the NATO alliance and the safety of the American nuclear umbrella. This, as the archbishop of London correctly put it in the church discussion of the Bomb, would be tantamount to asking that others sin. (We would add that hypothetically we would be asking that others perish for us.) This argument, with all its obvious hypocrisy, is very often just a midway stop before open neutralism. The latter can very rarely be assessed morally. As long as an alliance exists, however, a (not uncritical and not unconditional) loyalty to it is binding; otherwise we merely lend support to a Machiavellianism of the worst kind.

The second moral implication of the deterrent concerns its cost, which many see as indefensibly wasteful of resources that could be spent elsewhere. This dilemma has two facets. The first is very vulgar but, in a practical sense, extremely effective: there are very real, budgetary limits that constitute one of the major obstacles to the development of what is otherwise widely advertised as the independent European nuclear deterrent. Morally, such an argument is very simple to answer. If people believe (which seems improbable for other reasons) that a European deterrent furnishes the only means adequate to safeguard their freedom and yet are not ready to pay for it, they deserve what they get if worst comes to the worst. However, there is a more sublime argument. *Others pay*, so the argument runs, with their famine, underproduction, dependent economies, and the like, for our highly sophisticated weapons. Economically speaking, this may or may not be true. There are, in fact, valid arguments against a conception that computes the price of modern weaponry in dollars and then simply translates the sum total into the language of the absence of food, medical services, and schooling in vast regions of the world. Production for specific purposes is not something simply computable in dollars, as it presupposes a vast array of social preconditions that aid the production of certain goods that exist in the West and which are absent elsewhere. There are others, of course, who deny the force of this argument. We do not wish to take a stand here on the validity of either position, in particular as we have strong doubts about the feasibility of a European deterrent.* Even assuming such unfeasibility, however, if one attributes a value to freedom in one's own world, if one further believes that it is threatened, and if one regards the deterrent as morally acceptable, then it is surely one's duty to approve the economic sacrifices implied by the deterrent precisely because it is seen as a necessary safeguard for liberty.

However, there is an interesting *moral* argument against the deterrent to which an unpublished paper of Dusan Velickovic ("The Modern Meaning of Traditional Perpetual Peace Projects," 1981) alerted us. The author argues that while in the mainstream of European political thought, from Aristotle to Hannah Arendt, it has been consistent and valid, as long as the essence of politics did not degenerate into it, to regard violence as one of the means of politics, with the entrance of the nuclear deterrent, *perpetuated violence* has come to occupy a seemingly permanent position at the very heart of politics. It is in this sense that Velickovic speaks of the deterrent (for others it is the armaments race) as "perpetuated war." Being at the "heart of politics" means in more prosaic terms that potential violence in the form of the deterrent (perpetuated potential violence) plays an overwhelming role not just with decisions in areas that have traditionally been governed by the use of violence (such as conquest) but also in ones that traditionally have not included violence in principle. This indeed signals the serious moral degradation of contemporary politics in general.

But in what sense does the deterrent (as perpetuated potential violence) differ from the role that has frequently been played by various kinds of weapons in previous histories? There are two distinct features of the deterrent in this regard. First, all weapons up until now, however revolutionary they may have proved in the history of warfare, have been accommodated into various types of politics that were governed by social strategies and not by weapons. The latter were tools, not policy makers. Today, the reversal of roles is not absolute, only relative. We would emphasize our earlier argument: it is society that pronounces the final word on the Bomb, and not the Bomb that dooms

*It is important to us that it was a passionately unilateralist antinuclear theorist, Alan Roberts, in one of the best articles written on this subject ("Preparing To Fight a Nuclear War," *Arena* [Melbourne] 57 [1981]: 45–93), who argued that it is dilettantish to compute the costs of nuclear armament in dollars and simply "transfer them to the account of the poor regions."

society. However, there is indeed a relative reversal of roles in the sense that the Bomb does predefine certain policies as feasible, others as nonfeasible, and creates political options that hitherto have not existed. (There was only one predecessor to this: the introduction of the modern air force and the early versions of rocket warfare, which for the first time in history made available the hitting of an unarmed populace in nonoccupied territories as a genuine military option, thus opening possibilities for new kinds of policy.) Second, with all the endless wars of human history, peace and war have always remained sharply distinguishable concepts. This has now been relativized by the deterrent: when the means of maximum warfare is the guarantee of peace, the conceptual distinctness has indeed been blurred. Relativization is, however, not identical with disappearance. To state that the deterrent (or the armaments race), the perpetuated *potential* violence, is *actual war* is an inadmissible exaggeration, sometimes a sign of theoretical hysteria. There is a very good distinction between potential violence, perpetuated or otherwise, and war: in the latter, people are killed actually, not potentially. But with all this, the moral objection made to deterrence is genuine and serious at the same time, one with which present humankind has to coexist.*

What kind of arguments does the practical criticism of the deterrent entail? The basic practical argument is that the deterrent is dysfunctional while at the same time it enhances danger. This assertion can have two meanings: that the deterrent has either always been or just recently become dysfunctional. The possibility of such a loss of functionality cannot be denied. In fact, we have already mentioned two social conditions, the lower and the upper level (a level where there is no longer resoluteness to use the deterrent and, alternatively, a level where there is a necrophile eagerness to use it), at which the deterrent becomes dysfunctional. A third condition should be added to these: the deterrent is no longer functional when it is not regarded as universal, in other words, when people living in a region have the feeling that they are going to be victimized in a *limited nuclear war*. This question has an extreme political relevance as Europeans (and above all Germans)

---

*In our view, Michael Walzer summed up the problematic of the deterrent succinctly and correctly in the following words: "Supreme emergency has become a permanent condition. Deterrence is a way of coping with that condition, and though it is a bad way, there may well be no other that is practical in a world of sovereign and suspicious states. We threaten evil in order not to do it, and the doing of it would be so terrible that the threat seems in comparison to be morally defensible." Michael Walzer, *Just and Unjust Wars* (New York: Basic Books, 1977), p. 274.

show a perfectly natural resistance to being placed at the front line of a limited nuclear war that would destroy them while the United States remained unscathed. The feeling is rooted not only in the morally unacceptable American monopoly over the use of the weapons but also in the contradictory statements of American politicians, leading members of the civilian and military establishment who sometimes confirm, sometimes deny the alternative of a limited nuclear war. Precisely for this reason it is important to quote at some length from a paper by a leading expert, Desmond Ball, which deals with the controllability (and therefore the limited or inevitably unlimited character) of nuclear war:

> To the extent that there is a typical lay image of a nuclear war, it is that any substantial use of nuclear weapons by either the United States or the Soviet Union against the other's forces or territory would inevitably and rapidly lead to all-out urban-industrial attacks and consequent mutual destruction. . . . Among strategic analysts on the other hand, the ascendant view is that it *is possible to conduct limited and quite protracted nuclear exchanges* in such a way that escalation can be controlled and the war terminated at some less than all-out level. Some strategists actually visualize an escalation ladder, with a series of discrete and clearly identifiable steps of increasing levels of intensity of nuclear conflict, which the respective adversaries move up and down at will. Current US strategic policy, although extensively and carefully qualified, is closer to this second position. . . . The notion of controlled nuclear war-fighting, [however,] is essentially *astrategic* in that it tends to ignore a number of the realities that would necessarily attend any nuclear exchange. The more significant of these include the particular origins of the given conflict and the nature of its progress to the point where the strategic nuclear exchange is initiated; the disparate objectives for which a limited nuclear exchange would be fought; the nature of decision-making processes within the adversary governments; the political pressures that would be generated by a nuclear exchange; and the problems of terminating the exchange at some less than all-out level. Some of these considerations are so fundamental and so intemperate in their implications as to suggest that there can really be no possibility of controlling a nuclear war. . . . The likelihood that effective control of a nuclear exchange would be lost at some relatively early point in a conflict calls into question the strategic utility of any preceding efforts to control the exchange. . . . Furthermore, the technical and strategic uncertainties are such that, regardless of the care and tight control which they attempt to exercise, decision-makers could never be confident that escalation could be controlled. Given the impossibility

of developing capabilities for controlling a nuclear exchange through to favorable termination, or of removing the residual uncertainties relating to controlling the large-scale use of nuclear weapons, *it is likely that decision-makers would be deterred from initiating nuclear strikes no matter how limited or selective the options available to them.**

What can we learn from this expert opinion? First, that, despite all statements of politicians to the contrary, American (and in all probability, Soviet) strategic thinking *does* consider the possibility or option of a limited nuclear war. In exposing this dangerous thinking, the anti-nuclear movement does great service to European people: we simply have to know what kind of strategic games are being played with us, even if only hypothetically. But, second, from here the expert proceeds through a number of very technical considerations to the conclusion that it is precisely the strategic premise of a so-called limited nuclear war, namely, the controllability of such a war, that cannot be assured as a result of factors that follow from the total character of modern war, and which cannot be either programmed or kept in check by strategic thinking and acting alone. Third, expert thinking arrives smoothly from here at the rediscovery of the idea of the deterrent: given this uncertainty of controllability, the author contemplates, the decision makers will refrain from using nuclear weapons. The problem, however, is that what is a smooth transition in theory is a very complicated issue in practice. As the deterrent is dependent on its being a credible (potential) force—on the credibility of the determination to use it— once people realize that what the politicians tell them to reassure them and what politicians and military experts actually consider to be genuine options are not identical, credibility (or determination) evaporates and the deterrent ceases to function. Therefore it would be a highly practical objective of reasonable political movements to demand, among several other things aimed at the total structural rebuilding of the Western alliance, the public *and* secret abandonment of any idea of a limited nuclear war. This is an American duty and responsibility, but it obviously has important European ramifications. However, proceeding from here to state (as Joan Lestor, among others, has done in the British debate) that the Bomb has no deterrent function is, if the statement is projected back into history, totally to mystify postwar European history. Should one further maintain that because of the intense competition between them, the superpowers are inevitably on a collision

*Desmond Ball, *Can Nuclear War Be Controlled?*, Adelphi Papers No. 169 (London: International Institute for Strategic Studies, 1982), pp. 35, 36, 37. Italics ours.

course (and if one does not maintain this then what is the whole antinuclear issue about?), and should one also assume that it is not the nuclear deterrent, alone or overwhelmingly, that to date has prevented a nuclear confrontation, then we confront a truly unresolvable puzzle.*

In another version, people accept the functionality of deterrence in the past, but they argue that it has ceased to function as such; it is no longer a deterrent. The explanations are generally so confused that they are better understood the other way around. It is not the alleged loss of the functionality of deterrence that accounts for the idea of an imminent nuclear war, but the obverse. Since people in huge numbers have come, because of wider social considerations, to believe that we are nearing a nuclear war (an ''end of the world'' or, more precisely, the end of a particular world), therefore they no longer believe in the deterrent's functionality. As we have rejected the latter view, we are only consistent if we reject the former. For us, there are still no reasons to deny the functionality of the deterrent. There is, however, one fact that leads us to believe that the deterrent has been weakened, and, perhaps ironically, it is the antinuclear movement itself that is responsible for this. These days one can see a certain amount of disappointment, even resignation, in the ranks of the movement over their inability to prevent Pershing and Cruise missiles from being deployed in Europe. There is absolutely no reason for such resignation. The antinuclear movement is extremely powerful, but not, at least for the time being, in the sense of actually preventing governments from implementing certain military policies that are regarded as necessary to the Western alliance. The power of the movement lies elsewhere: in effectively undermining the deterrent, which is a social institution, not a technical gadget, which is dependent on the determination of people to use it in a hypothetical case. We do not intend to state that such determination, the criterion of credibility, is entirely gone, but it has been considerably weakened, and this represents an actual victory for the antinuclear movement but not necessarily a victory for freedom and life. We do not, however, want to throw the ball back into the other's court: we do not mean that, because the deterrent has been weakened, we have come closer to war. Nonetheless, new avenues have undeniably been opened for Soviet strategy.

*Assuming at least the past relevance of the deterrent, the whole story remains clear except one chapter: why did the Western allies not use the nuclear weapons between 1945 and 1949, when they had a monopoly as well as a superiority in carriers? The answer, we think, would be that, first, world opinion (including domestic public opinion) would not have accepted a preemptive nuclear strike, and, second, the strategists did not believe that nuclear weapons alone would have done the job, as they regarded the Soviet Army to be incomparably more powerful than the combined Anglo-American armies.

# III. The Soviet Strategy

What are our sources in assessing Soviet strategic policies? The question is more than rhetoric. If there is any methodologically suspicious element in predictive Kremlinology, it is the ostentatious display of too much inside information. In all reliable predictions the analyst departs from a definite view of the social character of the power under scrutiny and comes to certain conclusions on this basis and on that of one's political theory and anthropology.* Our analysis will not differ from this formula. We have set forth our view of Soviet societies in our book, written together with György Markus, *Dictatorship Over Needs*; accordingly, our predictions, based on publicly and widely known events and no behind-the-scene information, follow from this view of the Soviet regime.

In *Dictatorship Over Needs* we abandoned the traditional Marxist monist method (which deduces all spheres of societal life from the "basic" one, production) and thereby abandoned the category of the "mode of production" as well. We have sought to understand Soviet societies, as one fundamental version of modernity, in their totality, examining them on several different, but equally crucial, levels of understanding. We have argued that all Soviet societies are characterized by a double dynamic: an on-going, even expanding tendency to increase the material wealth of society (the Soviet regime is an industrial-modernizing one), at the same time expanding the control of the ruling apparatus. This overall *social telos*† yields the "goal of produc-

*If one casts a glance at such highly praised academic works as *Russia and the Road to Appeasement* and *Russia and World Order* by G. Liska (Johns Hopkins University Press), one will witness the same basic formula.

†The category is near Castoriadis's "imaginary institution," but it is not identical with it. We do not have space here to discuss the differences.

tion'' (and not the other way around): use value is socially defined in a "dictatorship over needs" by being part of this expanding material wealth and being subjugated to expanding social control. Both the social telos in general and the "goal of production" in particular promote an expansionist logic that cannot be described in terms of "imperialism" (the Soviet societies are not profit regulated and instrumental-rational) but which cannot exist without its expansionist dynamic. Almost all Soviet societies are industrial societies; in fact, the industrializing logic of modernity expands to extents that are inconceivable (as far as speed, social costs, and human "costs" are concerned) in liberal capitalism. If one needs a "material basis" to understand the general social telos of expansionism, excessive industrialization is such a material basis. While obviously no concrete step of Soviet foreign policy can be "deduced" from this universal constellation, the fact remains that Soviet societies cannot solve their inner tensions without expansion, nor can they ideologically legitimize their functions and modes of existence.

Soviet expansionism remained somewhat tarnished under the inwardly murderous and outwardly cautious first decade and a half of Stalin's rule. Its first signs only became visible during the Molotov-Ribbentropp pact. While this event can be interpreted in whatever way the interpreter wishes, the "minor blemish" of devouring Poland together with Hitler cannot be explained away: *it was the first act of Soviet expansionism*. Stalin, as shrewd as he was ruthless, went one major step further after the victory, and within three years he completed the occupation of Eastern Europe. Although his armies had moved deeply into Germany, however, he held Austria in a state of suspension and, while occasionally he neared various parts of Scandinavia, never made one further dangerous move. It is now a generally known fact that he even tried to discourage the Chinese communists from a final offensive because, as the most commonly accepted interpretation goes, he considered the Soviet Union to be too weak as yet to venture any further. This explanation could be entirely true, but as far as we can see, it has to be reinterpreted. There are few signs that indicate either that this concern was technological in nature or that Stalin had drawn major technological-strategic consequences from his devastating defeats during the first year of the war. The Soviet Army continued to suffer difficulties during Stalin's last years. Its best generals were either politely exiled (Zhukov) or used for political purposes (Rokossowski, who became "our man in Warsaw"). Several ideologically motivated bans on technological research and on the use of applied technology remained in force and slowed down development in military technology. (The most famous example is the ban on "bourgeois" cybernetics, without which modern warfare and military training are inconceivable.) Yet Stalin learned other lessons from the war. Official propaganda notwithstanding, he must have clearly known how shaky the foundations of the Soviet regime had proved to be during the war wherever the Soviet Army had pulled back from a region. He was also well aware of the extent to which Hitlerite brutality and ideological fanaticism had been needed to guide a jubilantly anti-Soviet populace back in the direction of a reluctantly pro-Soviet stance. He watched with even greater suspicion the newly occupied Eastern European countries. As the true creator of the regime for which expansion without all-embracing control was worthless, he must have felt that control had to be further strengthened and intensified; the new territories had to be absorbed and governed with an iron hand. In all probability, it was primarily the fact that social control was not sufficiently deeply rooted, not sufficiently all-embracing, rather than military considerations that commanded a halt to Soviet expansionism.

The new features, the whole novel framework of present-day Soviet expansionism, were designed under the confused and contradictory but historically crucial period of Nikita Khrushchev, in whose policies there was, despite undeniable contradictions and spectacular and seemingly irrational changes and improvisations, a much firmer consistency than is generally assumed. In the area of foreign policy Khrushchev is regarded, more often than not, as a shallow clown who liked to travel and behaved on his trips in an unstatesmanly manner, gave speeches on questions he was totally unfamiliar with, and took action with a degree of improvisation (from Berlin to Cuba) that thoroughly endangered the peace of the world (or, viewed from another angle, the well-considered interests of the USSR).

While the details can be correctly assessed, we find the verdict as a whole a complete misreading of Khrushchev's incomparably more complex political personality. In his autobiography, he narrates an extremely telling story which sheds much light on the origins and genuine objectives of his later foreign policy. As a pillar of Stalin's last Politburo but as a politician who, up until then, had hardly had any experience in foreign politics, Khrushchev had vigorously encouraged Stalin to display a full and open Soviet commitment to North Korea in the Korean War and give all the military aid "the Korean comrades need." It is clear from his own description that Stalin had fenced him off with a measure of disdain, giving him a few quick lessons in the basics of "socialist foreign policy." The conflict, obviously not serious for Khrushchev had survived, was largely one between two generations of Bolshevik functionaries. For Khrushchev, the postrevolutionary communist, the victorious Soviet Union was strong enough after the war to embark on its historical mission in the rest of the world without hesitation and double talk about noninterference, with all the external insignia of the liberator.* It is well-known how surprised John F. Kennedy was during their Vienna talks to hear, after the endless, albeit transparent, diplomatic lies of Stalin and Molotov, clear language from Khrushchev. The first secretary stated without camouflage that it was the "duty" of the Soviet Union to lend support—if need be even military support—to so-called wars of liberation everywhere. (Earlier it had been almost regarded as a crime against the state to assume that the Soviet Union had anything to do with any of the communist-led rebellions, revolutions, or partisan wars throughout the world: the "exporting of revolutions" was a Trotskyite idea.) In fact, the "struggle for peace" (the Khrushchev period abounded with his clamorous and wholly unrealistic offers of almost complete disarmament) and the insistence on the "world revolutionary process," on the "worldwide victory of communism," form one unitary process. The Soviet Union would not launch a thermonuclear war (Khrushchev seemed to have honestly believed in the universal destruction that would follow in the wake of such a war), but it would develop, whatever the costs, its nuclear strike force, in part as a deterrent (Khrushchev still faced a West that had guts and had not, at least not formally, resigned from the policy of "rolling back" communism), in part as a means of terror and blackmail. It would support uprisings and rebellions of *all kinds*. Khrushchev's great, then unacknowledged, invention was that he regarded Lenin's Machiavellian suggestion ("let us support the emir of Afghanistan who is more progressive than Kautsky because he is hostile to Western imperialism") a useful, operative idea. Following closely this principle, he decorated Gamal Abdel Nasser as a hero of the Soviet Union. It is less understood that his policy toward Yugoslavia was instigated according to the same principles. Not for a moment did he believe that Tito had "corrected his mistakes" (the resolution of the Soviet Communist Party on the intactly preserved revisionism of the Yugoslavs in the aftermath of the Belgrade meeting testifies to this).

---

*It is the just irony of history that toward the end of his political career Khrushchev met a new opposition, in the group of Mao, which charged *him* with too much caution and making too many concessions.

But for Khrushchev it was towing the Soviet line that counted, not ideologies, and he hoped, mistakenly, that Tito would tow that line. Maintaining the nuclear balance, increasing Soviet superiority to a point where its power could arouse fear and could be used as a means of bargaining without ever contemplating, however, the possibility of an all-out nuclear war; being able nevertheless to conquer the world through fear, to exploit weakness, subversions, and rebellions of any kind: this was and has remained the master formula of Soviet expansionism under all successors of Khrushchev.*

Everything that has happened after Khrushchev (and this statement now already covers two decades of Soviet expansionism) has to be understood, in our view, against the double, extremely complicated background of the increasing self-confidence and inner despair of the Soviet oligarchy. The self-confidence, which fuels their self-conceived historical mission of universal expansionism on all continents, is nurtured by three factors. First, the Soviet oligarchy feels, for the first time in Soviet history, that they have time, that they are not threatened with "running out of time." Second, despite all duplicitous lamentations to the contrary, the Soviet leadership does not have the slightest fear of the West. American military morale in Vietnam and the outcome of the Watergate affair (the near impeachment of an incumbent president is a sign for them of the contemptible weakness of Western democracies) were the last symptoms that were needed to convince them. Further, if the West was not able to attack them when it could have done so with a very good chance of winning and getting away with it, it would hardly do so now. Finally, they realistically know that there is no Western strategy, rather a progressively diminishing degree of Western unity.

Such increasing self-confidence would suggest strategic optimism, were it not more than sufficiently compensated by the inner despair, the result of the unsolved, protracted, and apparently insoluble inner crisis

---

*Admittedly, this continuity is not complete. Khrushchev was sometimes much too concerned with inner Soviet political stability to enforce budget cuts that the military resented and which have never happened since. He underestimated, inconsistently, the role of the surface fleet in an expansionist policy. His famous remark made during a visit to London testifies to this. There he suggested that the cruiser *Sverdlov*, on which he made his trip, could be purchased then and there, as only imperialist powers need gigantic fleets (a remark which would not have been to the liking of Admiral Gorshkov, now the head of perhaps the greatest single fleet in the world). However, these were inconsistencies *within* a policy formula that has remained valid.

of Soviet society, which can be summed up in the following terms. The Soviet oligarchy could have eliminated the most imminent danger of a general explosion following the death of Stalin, which threatened for three explosive years (1953–1956), from Berlin to Georgia, the edifice of "completed socialism" with "counterrevolutionary" explosions, by rejecting Stalin's murderous "revolutions from above." But they have never been able to achieve a genuine transition into a so-called intensive period of industrialization. Industry, except the military-industrial complex, works inefficiently and Soviet society remains technologically dependent on the West; the agricultural crisis cannot be overcome or compensated by an industrial boom; standards of living have been lagging far behind Western societies, and this is still true despite the longest depression capitalism has ever known. André Glucksmann sums up this situation in the following, picturesque way:

> The wind of spirit has turned. It is the West that makes the East dream. Bourgeois Europe has become the concrete utopia of the workers, peasants and intellectuals of Soviet socialist Europe. In 1945, the experts of the right despaired of, and the intellectuals of the left were enthusiastic about the idea that Western enterprises could be exploded by a revolutionary and communist ideology, while the system of private property was condemned to crises and catastrophes. Ever since, it is the turn of the masters of the Kremlin to denounce the fifth column which, in the inside of the factories, seizes the minds of workers and provokes "insurrectionist" strikes for such obsolete and formal rights as the freedom of opinion, right to assembly, the right to pray.*

In *Dictatorship Over Needs*, we analyzed the most dangerous internal and external enemy of the Soviet regime in a very similar way (except that we added the envy of Western affluence in sheer material terms to the complex). However, while we believe that this characterization is not incorrect, it certainly has to be complemented now.

Without a doubt, the Western way of life, and not the American Army, has remained the most powerful challenge for the nomenklatura, actually the only threat they are afraid of, and the one they wish to eliminate, for otherwise, as they believe, there can be no end to internal turmoil and unrest. But the subject in tacit disobedience (and sometimes in open revolt) that they are facing is now twofold. There is the aforementioned, the "fifth column of the Western way of life." But

---

*André Glucksmann, *La Force du Vertige* (Paris: Grasset, 1983), p. 52.

there is a novel one as well: *the anti-Soviet but anti-Western* Soviet Russian fundamentalist, the gigantic image of which can be found in Solzhenitsyn. In an act of statesmanship (which considerably surpasses the capacities that could have been expected from this power elite), the nomenklatura has come up with a twofold recipe against this new danger: the "Soviet way of life" and an updated version of Dostoevsky's "Russian idea." Both grow out of a situation in which the word "communism" has lost all seriousness, both at the top and at the social base. Victor Zaslavsky has analyzed in detail what "the Soviet way of life" means: paternalism and guaranteed security at the price of total depoliticization and automatic obedience, "order," the cult of authority and conservative ways of life, no social reforms or "improvisations," xenophobia with almost public anti-Semitism.* One has to add only a short quotation from Dostoevsky to understand precisely what the "Russian idea" means: "A truly great people can never reconcile itself to playing second fiddle in the affairs of humanity, not even playing an important part, but always and exclusively the chief part. If it loses that faith it is no longer a nation. But there is only one truth, and therefore there is only one nation among all the nations that can have the true God, even though other nations may have their own particular great gods."† If one were to translate Shatov's aggressive and laconic text into the banal language of present-day Soviet "literature," one would understand very well what is meant by the "Russian idea." However, the "Soviet way of life," the "Russian idea," and the ideological struggle against Westerners can achieve their aim only in the event of an utter humiliation, preferably total defeat, of the West. Therefore, expansionism remains vital for a system in crisis, even if the situation is incomparably more complex than Glucksmann's (or our own original) formulation suggested.

But if this is so, is it not reasonable to conceive *the Soviet Union as a military society*, a conception which would have been ridiculous under Stalin but which recently has gained an ever wider audience? It has found its best, deepest, and most ingenious formulation in Cornelius Castoriadis's *Devant la guerre* (Facing the War), which analyzes the Soviet Union in terms of a "stratocracy," a military society. Shortly after the book was published, Wojczech Jaruzelski and his way of "pacifying" Poland seemed to present a spectacular corroboration of the theory.

---

*Victor Zaslavsky, *The Neo-Stalinist State* (Armonk, NY: M. E. Sharpe, 1982).

†F. Dostoevsky, *The Devils* (Harmondsworth: Penguin, 1957), p. 258.

We shall present here our arguments in refutation of Soviet societies as military societies, but we wish to emphasize that there is absolutely nothing in Soviet societies that would interdict with the force of "historical necessity" a regular and visible military takeover. The ineptitude of the Soviet bureaucracy could reach such a level in internal affairs, the danger of general chaos could be so imminent, that the military, motivated as always by so-called patriotic considerations, could sweep party apparatchiks out of power. Such a turn would be clearly visible, however, and in our view it would have the inevitable economic consequence of restoring a market economy for the Soviet Union (with as much state supervision and protection as in many Latin American countries) and leading it to join the capitalist world market. Nothing like this seems likely to happen in the Soviet Union. No relevant signs forecast such a historic turn.

The advocates of a military society can argue in one of two ways. One is to state that the military now in fact occupies the dominant positions in the Soviet hierarchy, and that the Soviet Union is a military society in precisely that sense. There are frequent attempts made to interpret each and every Soviet politician as a direct or indirect representative of the "military complex," but the facts, which deny rather than corroborate the theory, are so obvious that this is to be regarded as the weak version of the theory. The strong and much more sophisticated version is argued by Castoriadis. According to him, and his theory of the "imaginary institution," there is not and will not necessarily be any "red Bonapartsky." No visible military takeover is needed to assume the actual existence of a military society: no statistical analysis of the members of the Central Committee is required to make this theory more convincing, whatever the findings. There is, however, a social "imaginary institution," the military conquest of the world, operative in the Soviet society, which works through agents regardless of the external contingencies of whether they wear a uniform or civilian clothes. In this sense, the Soviet Union of the last two decades has gradually been self-transformed into a "stratocratie."*

Our first argument against the theory is that the telos we have suggested lies within Soviet societies, namely, the expansion of socioeconomic control embodied in social structures and institutions, among others, the "goal of production," is at least equivalent to the imaginary institution Castoriadis argues for. At the same time, it ac-

*Cornelius Castoriadis, *Devant la guerre* (Paris: Fayard, 1981), in particular pp. 251–64.

counts for the whole of Soviet history, not just a chapter of it. Secondly, Castoriadis has never renounced his theory of Soviet society as a type of capitalism. If this is the case, either there is no need to posit any special telos or imaginary institution for expansionism, assuming that the military telos is a factor common to all capitalist societies (which is at least questionable), or there are some special structural elements in "Soviet capitalism" that make it a military society. These, however, have never been elaborated by the theory of "stratocratie."

The main question that any theory of the Soviet Union has to address is the following. If we conceive of the party bureaucracy, or apparatus, as the civilian-clothed agent of an impersonal military telos, which at a certain point must mean that it merges, even sociologically, with the army, can this apparatus fulfill all the roles generally ascribed to the party bureaucracy, internally and externally? We believe it cannot, for the following reasons. The political-universal image attributed to the party by itself is a constitutive element of the regime. The party apparatus is the leading stratum required by a political society (a society in which political ideas, goals, and considerations dominate all other life activities) for its longevity, while the military simply cannot fulfill the same functions. This means that if the party is to be reduced to the role of the civilian-clothed agent of the military, it cannot function as a party any longer. There will indeed be a vacuum as Castoriadis himself surmises, but the vacuum would have to be filled *in a public and visible manner*, not just clandestinely, thereby transforming political rule into military rule pure and simple. Further, one of the sources of legitimation of the party, and the basis of its capacity for integrating the Soviet regime, is its nonparticularistic character. All organizations, associations, and institutions of Soviet society are particular; only the party is general. It is judge, supervisor, arbiter over all particularities in a capacity it could never uphold were it to be degraded, even if "clandestinely," to the role of a civilian-clothed agent.

Secondly, and more important, the party is "international," the military is, perforce, national.* There is no such thing, not even in hypotheses or ideologies, as an "international army." An army is always the agency of a particular nation, and its rule over another nation is *overt occupation*. If the party were viewed publicly as the civilian-clothed agent of the military, the extension of the Soviet regime would be simply identical with overt foreign occupation. But is it not so

*The meaning of this internationalism is well known: "the internationalist support" the Soviet Army lent to its Hungarian, Czechoslovak, and other "class brethren" in the form of interventions.

now as well, some will ask. Our answer is that the situation is more complex. Except in East Germany, where they are a "legitimately" occupying force, Soviet agencies make serious efforts to achieve covert rather than overt forms of occupation. While in Eastern Europe the Soviet regime is indeed the result of continued Soviet occuption, this is not the case everywhere (for instance, Vietnam and Cuba). Nor are the integrating functions of the Soviet regime exhausted by the term "occupation." Therefore, even if the party were to keep its uniform in mothballs, it could not fulfill its international function as a civilian-clothed agent.

Further, there have been short periods in Soviet history in which some sectors, first of all the party apparatus, were militarized (most of all during collectivization, when "party armies" fought a desperate war against millions of kulaks doomed to destruction). But on the whole, the Soviet way of taming the disobedient could never be adequately described by the word "militarization." It is particularly so in the most recent phase of the "Soviet way of life." A militarized society has a martial culture with open contempt for peace, with an exaggerated emphasis on valor. Soviet society, precisely in the period covered by Castoriadis's analysis, is dominated by the pharisaical phrase of "love of peace," the flagellation of "warmongers" and "militarists." Further, all military regimes understand themselves by definition in terms of the dichotomy "military-civilian" which presupposes the existence of civil society of a kind. However, all attempts to validate the claims of the "military" (as an openly corporate entity) over the "civilians" to certain crucial prerogatives constitute an open challenge to the party's rule. Without such attempts a military society is inconceivable; with such attempts the political society of "dictatorship over needs" is equally inconceivable. Not even the relative but important socializing role of the Soviet Army, so correctly emphasized by Zaslavsky, could be understood in any sense other than in terms of socializing the youth within a framework established *not* by the army, but by the party oligarchy. Finally, we believe that while, as observed by Castoriadis, Zaslavsky, and others, the Soviet Army and its separate industrial complex represent a bulwark of rationality in Soviet society in that they operate according to rationalized standards, under the effective control of a consumer, and the like, this too can only be achieved because the army is part of the regime and not coextensive with its leading stratum, either directly or indirectly (through the "imaginary institution"). The regime as a whole, as it stands now, is not rationalizable.

All this is not, of course, to state that there have been no changes in the Soviet power structure in the last two and a half decades. Instead of personal tyranny, a collective rule of an oligarchy has emerged that has legitimated, even if not publicly, the role of certain influential lobbies and power brokers in presenting their relatively distinct interests and policy recommendations. Because of both its innerly rationalized structure and its more prominent role in the Soviet-American competition, the army comes out on top of the list of competitors. The relative proportions in this competition have, as we have tried to show, considerably changed, not primarily for technological reasons, but because of the lost strategic confidence in the West. In this altered situation, the role of the army, not as a means of all-out warfare but as a means of blackmail and the guarantor of each and every anti-Western uprising, coup, and revolution, has grown tremendously. As we have shown elsewhere, the legitimation of the Soviet regime after Khrushchev has been increasingly based on a paternalistic and nationalistic ideology (albeit the Soviet regime never would, and never could, give up its "internationalist" function). This also squares well with the heightened role of a powerful national army, the symbol of a "great nation." All this and several other factors cannot, however, alter the ultimate fact that the party has remained in power, although with a totally empty, entirely iconographic ideology. Failure to see this caused the pessimistic, tragic tone of Castoriadis's book, and not any "latent antihumanism" as his biased critics would maintain.

We now turn to a detailed analysis of the Soviet threat.

What exactly does the Soviet threat mean? Does it imply the goal of a global nuclear war on the part of the Soviet Union? The answer is negative, and we have analyzed the reasons repeatedly and extensively. The meaning of the threat is equivalent to asserting Soviet expansionism with global aspirations of *total domination*. Should someone deny this as a social and imminent tendency of the Soviet system, one would be theoretically compelled to give some very serious explanation about the fate of Eastern Europe.

Although they have never ceased to be interested in Europe, it was at the end of the 1970s that the Soviet leadership ostensibly returned to the idea of a primarily European expansion. Earlier, there had been few encouraging signs for them. The governments of the crucial countries, as well as the bulk of the opposition in those countries, were strongly pro-Atlantic, or at least clearly hostile to the Soviet Union. Eurocommunism, now a spent and failed attempt to provide an alternative, had nonetheless temporarily deprived the Soviet leaders of their two most influential and strongest allies, for which an emerging, entirely Stalin-ist, and, in relative terms, not insignificant Portuguese communism was no compensation. Francisco Franco's death offered no opening to the Soviet plans on the Iberian peninsula for a number of reasons—the king's determined stance for democracy, the socialists' growing influ-ence, Santiago Carillo's verbally energetic, even excessive, Eurocom-munism (which in the light of his new pro-Soviet turn has proved a mere ploy), and the like. The economic situation in Europe, although deteriorating in some countries faster than in others, nevertheless re-mained generally tolerable. Germany, the political center of the Euro-pean scene, has for many years remained unaffected by the gravest symptoms of crisis.

All this changed, for a number of reasons, in the late seventies, turing Soviet expansionism resolutely back to the European theater. It is a matter of special consideration to what extent any Russian leadership (Soviet or non-Soviet) has historically felt itself to be either culturally European or the bearer of a "special Russian mission." (There is a good deal of evidence to suggest that the centennial discussion between neo-Slavophiles and "Westerners" goes on covertly in Soviet cultural life.) But a decision on this question is one thing; denying a *traditional Russian interest in politically dominating Europe is quite another.*\*

\*One such attempt to deny this can be seen with Rudolf Augstein who, in the pages of *Der Spiegel*, relies on the authority of Roy Medvedev, the oppositional Khrushchevite historian who sometimes proffers a better apology for the regime than official chroniclers. Against this legend the following facts should be recount-ed. From the time (mainly under Catherine the Great) Russia began to modernize and "Europeanize" its bureaucratic system and social affairs, including its legisla-tive processes, a Russian political presence in European affairs, especially in Cen-tral Europe (by which we mean the areas now called Germany and Austria and re-lated parts of what was then the Hapsburg Empire) was clear, unambiguous, and menacing. It is the authoritative view of Albert Sorel that, in its early crucial years, the French Revolution was saved by the fact that both Austria and Prussia, fighting each other to partition Poland, were mesmerized and paralyzed by their common fear of Russia. After the collapse of Napoleon, when the legendary Cossacks were very materially present in Paris, two of *Metternich's*(!) main dilemmas (see H. Kis-singer, *A World Restored*) were whether the Russian army would return at all and, generally, how to terminate the "revolutionary" policy of Alexander I (where "re-volutionary" simply meant the upsetting of the conservative *status quo ante*). Ever since the French revolutionary wars, in which Russian armies and fleet fought in Italy and Switzerland and tried frequently to gain strongholds in the Mediterranean, Russian imperial interest in the disintegrating Turkish Empire and in the revival of more or less independent Balkan countries with strong pro-Russian loyalties (espe-cially Greece) has been explicit. In the 1848–49 revolutionary crisis, Russia served first as a general warning to the much too sanguinary revolutionaries in Germany and the Hapsburg monarchy and later as the actual savior of the monarchy against

A further consideration of the Soviet leadership that recommends a primarily European expansion is democratic-political in nature, what we would call its' "China syndrome." Here, the debacle in China must have provided at least some lessons for the Soviet leadership. Even if this learning process has not been extended to incorporate deeper sociological factors, it must have included at least one lesson: excessively huge masses of people cannot easily be absorbed and subjected to the leadership of the USSR, even where they live in a Soviet regime. To seek new additions to the (Russia-centered) Soviet system in faraway regions of the globe is distinctly unattractive because of the technological difficulties of feeding, controlling, and guiding such regions, particularly if they are heavily populated or extend across large territories.* Finally, seeking domination in overpopulated and underdeveloped areas carries with it obvious disadvantages even for Soviet expansionism, which is not a profit-motivated imperialism. The Soviet nomenklatura cannot solve the burning economic problems of a continuously bankrupt Cuba or a famished Ethiopia. How then could they solve the problems of a Sovietized Indonesia?

The prime objective of Soviet expansionism, then, is the Finlandization or, rather, Vichyization of Europe. (And no sneering of the antinuclear theorists would diminish the seriousness of the threat.) But why the second term? What justifies speaking of a European Vichy? Finlandization means, as everyone knew once upon a time, when it was not yet an almost honorable title, limited sovereignty. The term derives from the limited sovereignty enjoyed by Finland. This involves a formal ban on Finland's participation in any treaty or organization which the Soviet Union regards as dangerous or damaging to its interests.

---

Hungarian republicanism. Louis Bonaparte was greeted, as newly elected president, as the happy medium between the "Reds" and the Cossacks, both actual French alternatives.

Although suffering a reverse in the Crimean War, after a second wave of modernization, the 1861 emancipation of the serfs, Russia was back in full swing at the center of Bismarck's strategic considerations. He simply could not imagine German unification without at least tacit Russian backing. All this has hitherto been common knowledge. It needed a unilateralist historical consciousness to create a legend of a Russia that is traditionally uninvolved in attempts at dominating European politics.

*Most of the Soviet satellites in Latin America and Africa are countries with small populations, some of them hardly bigger than a rocket launching pad or a naval base (and hardly used for any other purposes). As soon as Russian leaders have to deal with Soviet societies of a considerably larger population and with one not situated on the Soviet borderline (Vietnam and Vietnam-dominated Indochina), the leaders have to learn by their own bitter experience how unruly such dependencies are.

Presidents and governments of Finland, duly elected in free elections, have to be approved by the Soviet Union; indeed, elected governments have been dismissed because of the lack of such approval. There is an almost equally formal limitation imposed on freedom of press in Finland. The Soviet Union does not allow the Finnish press to criticize it. (Thus, when the press revealed the condition of the port cities after the Soviet evacuation, there was such vehement protest on the side of the Soviet Union that the reports had to be cancelled.) Within this framework, the Finns can freely live the life of a liberal parliamentary political system and a market economy. Such conditions are "not too bad," argue some Western Leftists who otherwise regard the introduction of identity cards as the absolute proof of 1984. Others would argue that our sovereignty under American hegemony is limited as well, so why the fuss? We reject this identification precisely in the name of a Left that has to be freed, once and for all, from an already traditional hypocrisy. American hegemony means, beyond any doubt, a supremacy over nuclear weapons that are American-made and American-financed but stored in Europe, a system which in its present form is unacceptable for Europeans of all persuasion and common sense but which is not identical with American use of such weapons ad libitum. Second, it means that one country, which was formally the loser of the Second World War and which still does not have a peace treaty, suffers from certain limitations imposed on its armament policy, and this is, indeed, a certain limitation of sovereignty. Third, it means that each administration of the United States did, and will do, everything in its power (financially, politically, as well as through its clandestine channels) to reverse all political decisions unfavorable for America, and in doing so, it will mostly follow egoistic American interests (as the U.S. role in the Greek colonels' coup or in the Turkish regime demonstrates). But American hegemony does not mean the formal right to dismiss governments disliked or mistrusted by the U.S. administration (not only social-democratic governments but the presence of Stalinist French communists in François Mitterand's cabinet testify to this). Further, it does not mean that the United States can impose its will on any major (or increasingly, even minor) European country if it is determined to make an anti-American decision. If one needs proof, one should think of the break of Gaullist France with the Western alliance. Antinuclear propagandists who find all media channels open to their anti-American propaganda are the best persons to decide whether there is any (formal or informal) obstacle to propaganda in Europe hostile to America.

However, "Finlandization" as an exceptional solution (which would certainly still be a dream for Eastern Europe) rests on three special factors. Finland, despite its political regime, was not part of the victorious democracies. For very clear historical reasons, it unforgiveably sided with Hitler; even if it was Hitler's strangest ally, only the flexibility of its political elite (which managed to change sides much earlier than the shrewd Rumanians) saved it from sharing the fate of the Eastern European countries. Second, Finlandization has remained what it is and not worse, namely, complete Sovietization, because not only the Scandinavian countries but also the United States, which felt obliged to show loyalty toward the small country, protected it against Stalin. Finally, precisely because of the above two factors, there is a *national consensus* in Finland guaranteeing the conditions of a peacefully limited national sovereignty. This is a consensus that today seems to be shared alike by ultraconservatives (who know that they cannot get better) and pro-Moscow communists (who know that perhaps even the Soviet Union would not be happy if they now upset the equilibrium). We are entitled to speak of the Vichyization rather than the Finlandization of Europe above all because such a national consensus about the self-limitation of national sovereignty cannot be attained peacefully in any other country, and therefore it has to be imposed coercively. *In fact, the slogan "better Red than dead" is a call for civil war*, between those who are either Red or would prefer to be, and those who would prefer death to this alternative. The parties could never find consensus (exactly because of the manner in which the question is posed), therefore the goal would not be a peaceful Finland but a European Vichy, with national KGBs or Gestapos. Further, "better Red than dead" in itself means more than the slogan of "Finlandization," as careful reading will show. "Finlandization" means the serious limitation of national sovereignty; "better Red than dead" is an injunction to submit to an alien, hostile *social system*, which is regarded even by those who coined the term as something very negative. Such a submission never takes place without the brutal crushing of huge social groups who would prefer death to being "Red" (whatever this connotes). And if someone thinks that such alternatives are purely hypothetical, one should think of the boat people of Vietnam, who indeed risk no less than death when they take to the sea in their miserable vessels. Finally, for "Finlandization" to be relatively mild, there must be a West European and American background that supports Finland, or at least, to formulate it more accurately, the opinion of which, for the time being and for one reason or another, is taken into consideration. In the case of the Finlandization of the whole of Europe, such a protective background would no longer exist, and therefore there would be no restraint on the part of the victors.

What are the objectives of a long-term "Vichyization" of Europe as the Soviet strategic goal? First, the expulsion of the United States from Europe, preferably by the Europeans themselves. This would be a resounding political victory for the Soviet system, the trigger to a political crisis of unheard of dimensions within the United States itself, and it would establish the Soviet Union in a political position just as unchallenged, or perhaps even stronger than, that of the United States in 1945. This would mean a total reversal of the results of the Allied victory, a landslide power shift without a war.

Second, Vichyization would transform a considerable and highly developed part of the capitalist world market into the "catering periphery" of the Soviet world system.* The Soviet leadership has very good reasons for wanting to achieve such an end: they have simply been unable to negotiate the transition to an "intensive period of industrialization" with its accompanying material benefits. At the same time, while "the perfecting of the economic system" is constantly splashed across the headlines of Soviet newspapers, even the vaguest ideas of genuine economic reform are regularly dismissed. This is so in part because there is no longer unanimity concerning what precisely such reforms would mean. The simple formulae for reform, seemingly panaceas after the total irrationality of Stalin's world, proved worthless, or only extremely relative palliatives. As well, there is a constant and strong fear of social change of any kind in an immobilist oligarchy: they are suspicious of experiments, which invariably bring "counterrevolutions." However, exporting the economic reforms, in the form of subjecting the industrial giants of Western Europe to the political predominance of the Soviet Union, bullying them into conditions that are advantageous to the Soviet leadership, would be an ideal solution. For the time being, it is entirely idle to speculate or "predict" whether such a transformation could in the end be achieved through an extremely narrow-minded Sovietization of the West European economies (which would destroy precisely the preconditions of their present effectiveness), or whether it would be a "Finlandization" in the strict sense,

---

*This statement means by definition that we do not share the thesis of Immanuel Wallerstein and others that there is only one world system, the capitalist. We shall develop our thesis in a forthcoming study.

in that a functioning market economy subsists but under political dictates. Indeed, such speculation would hardly just be idle, but would be pernicious as well: "dreaming the dreams after defeat" is support lent to a future occupation. Nonetheless, the strategic objective seems to be extremely realistic.

Third, Vichyizing Europe would also mean a *cordon sanitaire* around rebellious Eastern Europe. A Vichyized Europe, even without the direct assimilation of the Soviet system, would be a very effective means of final (or at least a lasting) pacification of turbulent Eastern Europe. However much East European nations have known that they could not expect anything substantial from the West, there has always remained the faint hope that the West (and, in a geographical and perhaps economic sense, above all Western Europe) is ultimately sympathetic to their aims, and that in the unlikely case of a country's withdrawal from the Warsaw Pact they could rely on this sympathy in several respects. A Vichyized Europe would be a hostile environment for East European emancipatory movements, which are in any case facing an adversary with incomparably more powerful means. Finally, Vichyization would create an ideologically favorable atmosphere around the Soviet Union, which, as an ideologically constituted system, has always been very vulnerable to ideological criticism and "subversion."

This too, however, is already part of the present, in the form of a voluntary and anticipatory self-Finlandization. In Germany, Rudolph Bahro can be credited with embracing the "Finlandization option" of his own will. When one sees similar symptoms, however, from the authoritative writer and anti-Fascist Günter Grass, who is undoubtedly in the mainstream of public opinion and not the *enfant terrible* of *Nationalbolschewismus*, one has to realize that the process has indeed gone a long way already.*

---

*See Bahro's statement in *Le Nouvel Observateur,* June 26, 1982, p. 37. G. Grass said the following to *Newsweek* on September 5, 1983, p. 52: "In the long run we should aim at developing a new security system, a nuclear-free zone, for example, that would make NATO and the Warsaw Pact unnecessary. If that is 'neutralization' or 'Finlandization,' I say, 'Why not?'. I admire the Finns, these people who have managed to preserve their independence in spite of their long and open border with the Soviet Union." Grass is as ruthlessly outspoken here, as in his earlier, overwhelmingly anti-Soviet period. He hardly beats about the bush, and as it is very unlikely that he would not know *what kind of independence* the Finns are able to preserve, we can see a glimpse of a new Europe that embraces Soviet predominance for more limited gains (or illusions), nationalist in nature.

How should we imagine the Soviet *marcia su Europa?* The sarcastic antinuclear critics of NATO war games are certainly correct, partly because things almost never happen in the way strategists preconceive them on their computer or television screens, partly, and more importantly, because there is one particular scenario, precisely the one most analyzed by the NATO analysts as the unlikeliest course of future events: a frontal assault, conventional or nuclear, against one or all of the major West European countries (West Germany, France, Italy, and Great Britain). Let us repeat again and again: there is absolutely no necrophile element in the intellectual make-up of the Soviet apparatus. While it is undoubtedly true, and a source of great internal NATO tensions, that, as Glucksmann put it, Americans in Dallas will not automatically die a nuclear death because Soviet tanks are in Frankfurt, nonetheless, such an assault is the most probable trigger to an all-out nuclear world war. As things stand now, and as long as the Western alliance exists at least in name, it would be almost impossible for an American administration to convince American public opinion of the superior wisdom of standing by idly while one of the major West European countries is destroyed and occupied. But the alternative is only nuclear war, gradually or directly.

Therefore it is the *southern flank*, the soft underbelly of Europe, where we can expect, under circumstances favorable for the Soviets, the most vigorous Soviet actions. There are immediate and traditional Soviet strategic interests (first of all, gaining direct and unperturbed access to warm-water ports and to the Mediterranean); there are conflicts to be exploited, old debts and "grievances" to be settled; there are even allies they can rely on. The first, cautious step would be an internal Warsaw Pact affair to which the West could not object with too much vigor: the removal (by a coup or otherwise) of the clique of Nicolae Ceauçsecu and the establishment of a loyally pro-Soviet leadership, as well as a redeployment of the Soviet Army on the territory of Rumania. A logical further step would be the exploiting of two major Southern European tensions: the Greek-Turkish and the Yugoslav-Albanian conflicts. Local wars in both cases (encouraged clandestinely by Soviet diplomacy) would be, whatever their outcome, exclusively to the advantage of the Soviet Union, which would act as the main ally of one party (in the Greek-Turkish conflict, without a doubt, the ally of the former; in a Yugoslav-Albanian conflict by keeping their options open) and a supreme arbiter over all of them. Such a conflict, if wide enough and skillfully exploited, could lead to the following crucial results.

Turkey would be constrained (either in the Finnish way, that is, by a "lend-lease" agreement, or otherwise) to make the Dardanelles a free and uncontrolled channel for the Soviet fleet. (The "Sovietization" of Turkey would lead, in all probability, to a long and bloody partisan war, and here there would be no economic advantages for the Soviet Union, but certainly strategic ones.) Greece would be "Sovietized" or itself fall prey to temptations. The country has a relatively strong Communist party, the morality and "sociology" of which can be traced back to the unbroken self-confidence of the Stalin years (which is a more than adequate qualification for the political and police apparatuses that would be required for the task). Andreas Papandreou's Socialist party, a new creation without long traditions, under a popular, shrewd, and extremely demagogic leader in whom sincere anti-Americanism and anti-Turkish feelings blend with an insincere pro-Soviet stance, could not present a serious obstacle to this. There is a widespread and legitimate anti-American feeling in Greece because the decades of tyrannically conservative rule could never have existed, as part of the "free world," without overt American support, and the latter was a luxury even in terms of American strategy at the time. In addition, NATO's incapability or unwillingness to guarantee certain vital Greek interests against another NATO member is a further powerful factor weakening the resistance to Soviet expansionism. Such a turn could bring about the reunification with its Greek motherland of Cyprus (a small country but important as a potential naval base; it already has a relatively strong, absolutely pro-Soviet Communist party), an event which would undoubtedly raise the following question: as far as the Turkish minority is concerned, are we not going to face something similar to the Armenians' fate?

Soviet expansionism, interestingly, is likely to meet more obstacles on both sides in its attempts to exploit a potential Yugoslav-Albanian conflict. Both countries are traditionally jealous of their national sovereignty; both have, almost alone in Europe, a brilliant record of indomitable partisan wars against foreign invaders. It is worth considering whether the Soviet Union, facing a number of Afghanistans, would be ready to use tactical, "Hiroshima-scale" nuclear weapons for purposes of intimidation. Whereas all this is speculation, if one takes into consideration the historical morality of the nomenklatura, there can be little doubt of its possibility. They could even use the American argument, namely, that all this is necessary to defend Soviet lives. But the main lever would be utilizing the Yugoslav-Albanian conflict centered on Kosovo, which, if the Soviets wisely side with the Yugoslavs, would inevitably mean the collapse of Enver Hoxha's disobedient regime, the installation of a pro-Soviet leadership (not a complicated matter, for in all communist apparatuses, quite naturally, there must be a latent pro-Soviet faction). Lending a hand to Yugoslavia could result, particularly if accompanied by the application of some pressure, in Yugoslavia joining the Warsaw Pact (perhaps with some special guarantees and certainly with safeguards for its considerably different social structure).* Let us emphasize that if all this is handled with sufficient finesse (and Poland in 1981, the only resounding political victory of the Brezhnev era in Eastern Europe, demonstrated that certain lessons have indeed been assimilated), the West can only stand by and observe events (including such additional moves as the incorporation of Malta into the "Soviet naval line of defense") in a state of immobility. As things stand now in Western Europe and America, the West would not be in a position to act otherwise.

There is only one region where resolute direct, overt Soviet expansionist action is imaginable: ironically, in Finland. As its fate has constantly hung precariously in the balance, as soon as the Soviet leadership is convinced that the nuclear deterrent has been sociopsychologically eliminated and conflicts within NATO are vehement enough, the Sovietization of Finland will take place, accompanied by some lively but peaceful and short-lived inner protests. The Finns, who have no great confidence in Western valor, are not likely to put up an excessively heroic and costly armed resistance without potential allies. No further moves would be expected in the immediate aftermath of the Sovietization of Finland against the core of Scandinavia: Sweden, Norway, and Denmark. The first is one of the two symbolically neutral countries of Europe; violating its integrity would provide only harmful publicity. The two latter are members of NATO (while Greece is only partially under the Western umbrella) and "organically Western countries" with traditions of liberal regimes. Their ill fate could provoke unexpected West European or American reactions.

---

*This would not be a totally unattractive outcome for the Soviet Union. Similarly, in an interview (of course, more propagandistic than sincere), Muammar al-Qaddafi of Libya has suggested his readiness to join, under duress from the West, the Warsaw Pact. There was no official Soviet response to this, for "the time is not yet ripe." But we can see absolutely no theoretical or practical obstacle for Qaddafi to do so, in which case he would become a comrade, and East European functionaries would be indoctrinated with the view that the "Libyan comrades" have their special, and certainly temporary, reasons for engaging in such irregular practices as the Moslem way of life.

Such vigorous movements on the southern and northern flanks by the Soviet Union would complete a gigantic pincer maneuver and leave Europe wide open to any military move, if need be, from any direction, and would inevitably place the Mediterranean under Soviet dominance. This having been completed, there are three weak spots of the Western system where the Soviet leadership could attempt political pressure combined with military blackmail. Holland, for reasons that are beyond our comprehension, is obviously the weakest spot of the Western alliance. The antinuclear movement there has become, in relative terms, the strongest contingent within the European movement. It embraces all parties, political positions, and avenues of life. Clearly, a country in which the soldiers of the army demonstrate in uniform against their main ally is, for all practical purposes, a member of the alliance in name only. If in an hour of national crisis the Soviets are shrewd enough to offer one of their endless and meaningless treaties of mutual nonaggression (and a leadership that firmly believes in the Turkish principle of politics—an oath made to the giaour is not binding—can easily do so), it would propel Holland out of the Western alliance toward a Swedish position, which would be a resounding political victory for Soviet strategy.

The second, always open field of expansion is Portugal, which for many reasons has not been economically or sociologically stable since the 1973 revolution. Its moderate and democratic military officers have up until now saved it from a totalitarian takeover, and the hold of the military over the civilian society, a danger in itself, irrespective of the eventual political affiliation of the army officers, has been considerably weakened. However, with an unrepentantly Stalinist communism still strong, a coup or even a civil war can never be entirely excluded. While all this would happen closer to the heart of the West, the degree of Western commitment to resisting such an eventuality is still not clear.

Austria is the last possible direct target. The neutrality of the country was the greatest, perhaps the only, concession the Soviet Union has ever made to the West. For almost thirty years now Austria has cautiously observed Soviet strategic interests and only touched upon Soviet sensitivities with gloved hands. There is absolutely no inner support for any pro-Soviet turn in the country: the antinuclear movement is insignificant, social democracy is firmly antitotalitarian. The Soviet leadership has in fact "Finlandized" Austria in the sense that the country's abstention from alliances is not optional but mandatory. Further, its Finlandization, or the formal ability to influence the internal affairs of the country, is not entirely excluded under circumstances favorable for the Soviet Union, but it is highly unlikely.

In Europe, however, everything depends on Germany, and in the last three to four years we have witnessed what earlier would have been totally unexpected—an explicit German nationalist upsurge, which is increasingly cross-class, transcends ideological barriers, and unifies even traditional enemies who for decades have not been able to sit down at the same table. *Der Spiegel*, with a pathos somewhat incongruous with the language of its otherwise ironical, cynical journalism, recently stated that the movement has created a national unity on the missile issue unparalleled since the national unity movement in 1848. The current national unity movement is, in an extremely heterogeneous orchestration but ultimately *unisono*, anti-American and extremely understanding toward the Soviet Union. Symbolically, during the huge October 1983 demonstrations all over Europe against the deployment of the Pershing and Cruise missiles, Soviet television did not show pictures of the massive Italian demonstrations (for at least the slogans there were evenhanded). On the other hand, they televised *without distortion* the German demonstrations, which only protested the presence of American missiles in Europe. Does this mean that we have to do with a gigantic "tacit collective conspiracy"? Is the antinuclear issue, which a decade ago was weak and insignificant in West Germany (in contrast to Great Britain) and has now grown into this tidal wave of enthusiasm, a Trojan horse behind which there is an awakening new Germany eager to be released from bonds and have its own nuclear freedom? This view, which has begun to emerge in various parts of Europe, above all in French public opinion, which is traditionally sensitive about German nationalism, is certainly a crude sociological simplification. However, let us quote from a splendid article to demonstrate that even according to German testimonies it has a considerable basis in reality:

> NATO's double decision focused public concern on two issues: the sovereignty of both German states and their populations' chances of surviving a limited nuclear war. The extent to which the reactions to these issues have a nationalist character can be ascribed to elder spokesmen of the SPD who, while not part of the peace movement, influence it nonetheless. Participants like Hellmut Gollwitzer and Heinrich Albertz sound very much like Guenter Gaus and Egon Bahr. . . . Bahr and Gaus argue that reunification and, ultimately, the restoration of national identity should be German politics' immediate concern: "if a German tells you that the

national question is no longer important, do not be so sure. Do not believe him. Either he is dumb or he is not telling the truth, and both positions are dangerous."*

It is precisely this covert and inauthentic character of the new German nationalist upsurge that causes immediate concern for the observer. The proof of a sudden change is beyond doubt: all analyses of the antinuclear issue conclude, either directly or with a detour, in establishing the moral and political foundations for German reunification. (Grass's interview mentioned earlier proceeds directly from the condemnation of American missiles and a very reluctant allegiance to the Western alliance to a nuclear-free zone in Europe, which is, to all intents and purposes, identical with the process of confederating the two Germanies.) The general social discourse, except on the aggressive Right, has changed dramatically as well. The leading liberal journals (*Die Zeit*, *Der Spiegel*), without weakening their traditional total contempt for "socialist utopias," have become excessively uncritical toward the Soviet Union and its East European empire and harshly critical of the United States, in the case of *Der Spiegel* very often in the tone of a traditional "cultural superiority." Jaruzelski emerges from their pages as the savior of Europe, the man who prevented an unruly population from triggering a world war (which is as far from historical reality as any German historical legend could be); Kádárist Hungary emerges as the *ne plus ultra* of human freedom. The Hungarian Revolution of 1956, once the favorite child of liberalism, now appears in the presentation of David Irving, a "historian" who has termed himself "mildly Fascist," as a mob uprising serialized by *Der Spiegel*. And while the criticism of the United States, in particular for the policies it pursues in Central America, is entirely justified, it is a telling historical fact that many of its anticommunist and antitotalitarian critics in Germany needed this particular historical hour to understand that which has always been clear to any objective observer: the deep contradiction within American foreign policy between defending the global interests of world capitalism and defending democracy. The translation of this fact into the formula that "America betrays her ideals" is little more than a depiction of the late-coming self-illumination of the German liberal.

How did this nationalist upsurge come about? Any approach to the "German issue behind the issue," namely, national unity through the

---

*Sigrid Meuschel, "Neo-Nationalism and the West German Peace Movement's Reaction to the Polish Military Coup," *Telos* 56 (Summer 1983), pp. 119–20.

antinuclear protest, has to start with *la condition allemande* in 1945, when not only the Reich lay in debris, but the very right to be German, even more a German nationalist, had been questioned by all victims of Hitler's aggression. Our analysis suggests a different approach. First, we believe that admitting the legitimacy of every single nationalism other than the German, or watching it with exaggerated suspicion just because of what transpired in an earlier phase of German nationalism, is racism with reversed signs. Either no nationalism at all or each and every nationalism has to be historically legitimized as long as it does not aim, explicitly or implicitly, at the extermination of other human groups. Second, on the basis of a *radical theory of the recognition of all needs, individual and collective*, though not exploitative needs, the German need for a unified nation simply has to be recognized. Finally, annoyed observers of the reemergence of a German nationalism often miss the important point that there is a self-critical element in the very structure of the new German collective feeling: *it is the nationalism of the German nation, not that of a future German Reich.* Characteristically, while it is a constant German neonationalist argument that the populace of the GDR shares a culture in common with "West Germans," and that therefore, sooner or later, it has to share the same sovereign nation with them, no such argument arises, either on the political Right or on the political Left, concerning Austria or the surviving German pockets in other East European countries. In this respect, the lessons of the (probably last) German Reich seem to have been learned properly.

The best characterization of the German destiny after Hitler is given, in our view, in the document of a small group of "Titoists" and Trotskyites (the so-called Independent Labor Party of Germany) in 1951: "The contradictions between the Western capitalist powers and the Soviet Union led, through the occupation of Germany and *the absence of a German revolution*, to the partitioning of our country. The collectively conceived Potsdam decrees of the superpowers about the subjugation and exploitation of Germany did not prevent the victors from adjusting quickly their respective zones of occupation to the structure of their own countries. . . . The reunification of Germany must not be the political victory of either the SED-bureaucracy or the Western capitalists."* Here, the reference to a German revolution that

*Peter Brandt and Herbert Ammon, eds., *Die Linke und die nationale Frage* (Hamburg: Rowohlt, 1981), pp. 97–98. In what follows we take our documentation mostly from this volume. We radically disagree with the editors on all counts, but we regard their selections as the paragon of an objective and knowledgeable presentation of an extremely debatable and sensitive problem complex.

never came in from the cold is vital. In fact, a German revolution in 1944 seems to be the last historical moment when Germany could have escaped being partitioned by putting a resolute end through German acts to the shame and misery Germans caused to endless millions, by setting their own house in order and thereby protecting the old edifice. It is not our concern here whether such a German revolution was "likely" or "unlikely"; we only would like to point to theoretical possibilities. Germans on the Left have argued in the last decades that a great opportunity for a Leftist victory in 1945 was miscarried by conservative Anglo-American policies. If half of this claim is true, the adherents of the Left must have been there in 1944 in sufficient number to use July 20, or any other occasion, to turn the Nazi tide. This is all the more so as Nazism, despite its omnipotence on the surface, in 1943–44 must have already been very weak. In particular, in 1944 the writing was clearly on the wall: the German armies were in retreat, German cities lay in debris, almost all its allies—Fascist Italy, half-Fascist Rumania and Hungary, pro-German (or rather, anti-Soviet) Finland—had all deserted the Nazi cause, so many signs and facts that not even Goebbels' propaganda could reduce them to "hostile figments of a feverish fantasy." However, *unbewältigte Vergangenheit*, "the unmastered past," this hackneyed phrase of German self-understanding, again produced a miracle. The historical legend of the *Dolchstoss*, in November 1918, stabbing the knife in the back of one's own fatherland, the compulsory mythological explanation of the first monumental German defeat, worked as a negative categorical imperative. Millions, in particular on the Left, who hated Hitler as no one else, who expected no better fate than peril at the hand of Hitler's myrmidons or the victors and were therefore led not by fear but by despair, still did not act, when they could have for the last time with historical efficiency, because they were not prepared to take the stigma of patricide, the *Dolchstoss*.

It is, of course, extremely difficult to foretell with any degree of accuracy what could have been achieved by a victorious German revolution in 1944. But in all probability, the scenario would have been the following: an immediate and exemplary punishment by *German* courts of all culprits of Nazi crimes, which would have rid German conscience, once and for all, of the burdens and psychoses of guilt; the immediate evacuation of all occupied territories and an offer of armistice and preliminary negotiations of a just peace treaty recognizing German responsibility but protecting German sovereignty and territorial unity; the elimination of the misconceived demand of an *uncondi-*

*tional* surrender;* saving of the lives of millions, non-German and German, who perished in the last year of Hitler's necrophile rule. Of course, there was a chance that a Germany, after its victorious anti-Fascist revolution, would have been met with misunderstanding and that it would have gone under fighting and free. However, that would have created a historical "origin" for the German future, something to which all later German generations could have returned with heartfelt relief. Such a conclusion is highly unlikely, however, given that in the Western democracies there was, if in a manipulated form, a public opinion far from ready to accept disproportionate losses of human life for unrealistic purposes.

Once this historical moment for a German revolution was missed, partitioning became inevitable, and German history up until the present *has developed in antinomies that have been lived by the overwhelming majority of Germans as suffering*. What is felt to be suffering *is* suffering. Germans were lucky, however, in that the majority of their occupied territory and populace fell into Western hands, and not those of Stalin. Whether one applies bourgeois-liberal or genuinely socialist standards to the assessment of historical events, the fact remains that even Konrad Adenauer's extremely restrictive, conservatively liberal *Obrigkeitsstaat*, this paragon of the cold war West, was a measure of freedom when compared to Ulbricht's and Honecker's "real socialism," and if German socialism has a future, it only exists where there is at least a measure of freedom. In addition, the Western occupants learned at least one lesson from Versailles: exploiting and humiliating the bulk of the German population is simply bad politics. Therefore the West "donated" a liberal system to Germany (or imposed one on it). This, together with the extraordinary talent of the conservative and misanthropic statesman, Adenauer, comparable only to that of Charles De Gaulle, plus the efficiency of his cynical power elite, created what the world saw as a genuine miracle: the strange "victory" of a Ger-

---

*There can be little doubt that the demand for unconditional surrender was egoistically motivated. The Western allies, who never bombed the concentration camps, and Stalin, who did not care about his own soldiers, were not concerned about the victims. They wanted to grab what was up for grabs and do it unperturbed by German (or Japanese) voices of protest. Also, the clause seemed to guarantee (although it did not) that none of the parties would have clandestine negotiations with the enemy when it was about to collapse. Further, the proviso was counterproductive. M. Walzer, for instance, has argued that Hiroshima or the napalm bombing of Tokyo would not have occurred had the American leadership confronted Japan with more liberal demands.

many after a war without peace, which is the other face of the "German condition."

What can be said were the antinomies of the German situation after 1945, after the *de facto* partitioning? The first pair of antinomies was presented in the following option: either a collective passive resistance of all Germans against all occupying forces as a long-range policy or a collaboration with them on both poles. And here, there was indeed no third option. In fact, to our knowledge, no serious political factor appeared, either on the right or on the Left, that would have prompted the Germans in 1945 to opt for Gandhi's strategy of noncollaboration. There were indeed very good moral and political reasons against such a choice. First, democratic and socialist Germans, and often even religious Germans without any political creed, felt so deeply remorseful for the terrible crimes committed in the name of Germany and by German hands that they could not mobilize the necessary amount of self-assurance required by such a long-range boycott. They also felt that they would become stooges of a clandestine Nazi resistance manipulating them shrewdly from behind the scenes, which beyond any doubt could well have become the case. But it was also true that all the trumps were in the allied hands, and that the leaders of the victorious powers had already toyed with the idea of turning a defeated Germany into a new Carthage. An all-German boycott could have triggered an Anglo-American and Soviet reaction of this kind. With all this, it cannot be denied in retrospect that this would have been a relevant and adequate answer, a collective protest that, lacking the revolution of 1944, could have upheld the German claim to full sovereignty more adequately and perhaps more successfully than all later maneuverings of German politicians.

The other option inherent in the antinomy was accepting the politics, the strategy, the hegemony, and finally the social system of one of the victors. The embracing of a Western hegemony and alliance offered two possibilities. One was represented by an SPD led by Kurt Schumacher. In order not to appear biased, we simply accept Brandt and Ammon's description of Schumacher's policy as accurate:

> From now on, the line of Kurt Schumacher's has broken through permanently. Schumacher, who had spent 10 years in a concentration camp during the Third Reich, emphasized like no one else since the spring of 1945 the necessity of a radical self-purification and social change as the right of the German people to national unity and equal rights. At the same time, he criticized with unusual outspokenness the occupying powers, in

particular the USSR, so that he was regarded as a "nationalist." Apart from fundamental convictions, the underlying idea of Schumacher's patriotic rhetoric was also the fear that once again, as in the Weimar Republic, it could be the "false powers" (as in his view the communists and the Right were), who would exploit for their purposes certain existing national problems. Schumacher was convinced that Germany could only be reconstructed in a "socialist" way, and that German democracy had to be founded in a socialist manner in order to last; the socialization of fundamental raw materials and key industries as well as big banks belonged to this. Schumacher claimed the politically leading role for the SPD as the only undeniably democratic, freedom- and socialism-oriented, at the same time internationalist and patriotic party, which he wanted to realize in sharp confrontation with the bourgeois Right and Center parties and the communists. Above all, he made the reproach to the KPD and SED that they were oriented exclusively toward the interests of the USSR, instead of those of the German working people. For him, the USSR was a nondemocratic and nonsocialist state, while he saw socialist trends emerging in the Western states (New Deal, Labour governments). . . . From the start, Schumacher was West-oriented. . . . In contrast to Adenauer, he did not commit himself unconditionally to an alliance of the western zones of occupation with the West. Although he did not reject later the German contribution to defense in principle—at any rate, he combined it with unacceptable conditions—the emphasis of his conceptions has always been on the democratic and socialist "magnetic appeal" of West Germany to East Germany, instead of on military terrain.*

It is at this point that we can grasp the historical responsibility of the Western powers for the emergence of a conservative Germany for a period of two decades. This was the second possibility flowing from an

---

*Brandt and Ammon, eds. *Die Linke und die nationale Frage*, pp. 36–37. We identify with Schumacher's conceptions to a very great extent and simply cannot see any reason other than Brandt and Ammon's Leninism (within their "national Bolshevism") that would justify their using the term socialist in quotes with Schumacher. (For Schumacher's option meant accepting the Western alliance, but *not* the Western system.) In particular, we endorse fully his conception of the Soviet Union. Of course, a number of naïvetés could be pinpointed in this, as in all other socialist theories. However, his conception of a "new democracy," the radicalization of democracy, as the only path to socialism shows a remarkable similarity to the best that was invented by latently anti-Stalinist communists of the immediate postwar period, such as G. Lukács. And we find the type of criticism of Schumacher's conception to be found in Kluge-Negt, *Geschichte und Eigensinn* (Frankfurt, 1981), pp. 1093–1129, particularly unfruitful. The insistence on a "proletarian" character of socialist politics (whatever the term under modern conditions should mean apart from being a wage-laborer employed in the industry) does not add anything to a correct socialist strategy.

acceptance of the Western alliance. America was naturally mistrustful of the socialist conceptions of Schumacher as was, equally naturally, the British Tory establishment, whose political and military infrastructure was the *de facto* administration in the British zone. (And not even a victorious Labour found the determination, for nationalist reasons, to side with a natural ally.) It would be an exaggeration to say that the British and the Americans "suppressed" the socialist option (although they were all-powerful during those years and did everything to obstruct it). But the simple fact that Schumacher's strategy was for them clearly and publicly unacceptable, and not even negotiable, miscarried the chances of a radical social democracy from the start. The Western powers needed Adenauer, the anti-Bismarck, the man who had the moral courage to divide his own people in order to recreate its role as a powerful nation; who was, however, Bismarckian enough to tolerate government through parliament only to the absolutely necessary minimum degree. With this Promethean act of a conservative nation-creation barely four or five years after the war, an achievement nobody believed possible in 1945, a set of negative features that have never been eliminated or rectified emerged as characteristic of West Germany. First, and this is borne out by key documents of the West German trade unions from the Adenauer era, Adenauer's victory was not just accompanied by the emergence of an extremely restrictive and authoritarian state, hardly reformed later by social-liberal governments, but it also embodied the purest capitalist domination of economic and social life in liberal Western Europe. Of course, the reverse side of this situation has been a policy of gradually raising standards of living over a period of more than twenty years, during which West Germany has become the most prosperous nation of Europe. But the new German prosperity favored above all an ostentatious, repressive, and uncultured class of *nouveaux riches* whose roots go back to a shady prehistory during the Third Reich. Further, once a "donated sovereignty" has been accepted, and this is precisely why Adenauer enjoyed the confidence of the Western powers, there is no going back. Sovereignty is stipulated as a fact, never shaped in a nationwide consensus. Independence existed without a declaration of independence (just like peace without a peace treaty), and therefore it could be, and in fact has been, called a nonindependence; more particularly, a nonsovereignty. Statements such as these may be exercises in demagoguery or at least exaggerations, but they are certainly not lacking altogether in historical foundations.

Third, on this basis no peace treaty could ever be concluded. The end of the war, just as the beginning of sovereignty, was an act without ratified agreements, something of a mythological event whose interpretation is truly open-ended. Finally, consistent de-Nazification simply could not take place, and the reasons are deeper than just a series of cover-ups on the part of an archconservative establishment. Adenauer's West Germany was a nation that regarded itself as sovereign, but which had no instrument of sovereignty; a nation that regarded itself as defeated and dispossessed of a quarter of its territory by the USSR but was powerless in translating such perceived injustices into an outright condemnation of the terms of Germany's defeat because of the Western powers it had to rely on; a nation that was used and greatly favored as a political and military instrument against the USSR but which was, at the same time, publicly mistrusted; a conservative state that could hardly fool its own electorate about having postponed reunification *ad calendas Graecas*, and which, therefore, had to be extremely sensitive about the past and the deeds of that same electorate; in sum, Adenauer's West Germany, caught in the web of all such contradictions, could do little other than circumvent the "Hitler-syndrome" by a superficial rhetoric about barbarism, instead of radically eliminating at least those roots of Nazism that were incompatible with a Christian culture.

However, the alliance with or integration into the "West" of Adenauer's Germany has set in motion a new pair of antinomies. On the one hand, a "European," a "Western" Germany was hardly less of a rupture with German traditions than Hitler's, albeit a beneficial one. Politically, it meant a radical abandonment of any idea of a Reich. The CDU-CSU circles could make as much noise as they wished about expelled Germans, against the loss of territory on behalf of Poland and the USSR, but the *Bundesrepublik* would be no conduit for any messianic empire to come, rather an integrated (or, as Germans still tend to believe, overintegrated) part of an alliance. Culturally, it meant the far-reaching Americanization of West Germany, a trend which, of course, finally could not shake the self-confidence of what has remained one of the leading cultures of the world, but nonetheless a trend against which Germans now fight with good reason, even if often it is under the sign of questionable objectives. Most importantly—and today this is a typical criticism levelled on the Left against Adenauer's policy, but increasingly in the center (and perhaps soon on the Right) as well—the integration into the Western alliance, the politics of *Alles oder Nichts* meant a perhaps deliberate and certainly a final abandonment of German reunification (short of some miraculous turn in history like the collapse of the Soviet Union). The other side of this antinomic situation, however, is that this new Germany, which went the farthest in "self-Westernization" and the abandonment of the imperial idea, could not allay suspicion in either the East or the West. As far as the East is concerned, up until 1970 consecutive Soviet leaderships had played on the "danger of German revanchism." Of course, it is always difficult to determine whether such perceived threats are real or whether they are merely exploited for political purposes, but it is an indubitable fact that, excepting China and the "yellow peril," the only instance of a coincidence of government and popular perceptions in foreign policy in the USSR has been this common fear of a new German power. As far as the West was concerned, the rise of a new German power, however integrated, simply could not fail to trigger immediate French suspicions. The last years of the Fourth Republic were spent in nervous debates about the French role in NATO were West Germany to join it as a full-fledged member. There could be, and indeed there was, no mistake either in the United States or in the Federal Republic that the Gaullist decision to leave the military alliance was triggered to a very large extent by the German rise to quasi-independence. De Gaulle publicly warned about a complete French *volte-face* and, if need be, a revival of the traditional Franco-Russian pact, in the event of a German nuclear rearmament. West Germany has, then, remained the Western continental power par excellence, with all the burdens, risks, and duties that go with such a role, but without the trust and recognition that normally accompanies such a role within an alliance. This is indeed an antinomic situation for both West Germany and its allies.

A third set of antinomies came about in the relationship of the Federal Republic to the eastern part of Germany, which Adenauerian Germany, with an unusual lack of realism, kept calling SBZ (*sowjetische Besatzungzone*—Soviet zone of occupation) and was not prepared to regard as a state with at least formal sovereignty. There was, of course, more to this than just foolhardiness. It was integrally bound up with the whole system of *Ersatzlegitimation* of Adenauer's historical option. That he chose, via an "integration with the West," a particular German state which was the only possible German nation meant that he was necessarily bound to regard the rest of Germany as a Soviet colony. For a very long time the Adenauer propaganda worked not just because of the sheer brutality with which the Soviets handled the German question (in particular, we have in mind the tragedy of millions of

Eastern *volksdeutsche* who were expelled from their homes and native countries in the most horrendous way), but also because of the attitude of the East German apparatus itself, which, while wishing for the permanence of its position, was quite unsure about its master's intentions. In their quick justification of whatever atrocities were committed against German POWs and *volksdeutsche* Germans in the USSR and in East European countries, and their direct dependence on Soviet military commanders, the East Germans indeed resembled much more a colonial administration than even a subservient government. It was precisely the Adenauer solution, however, that had accelerated matters: the deeper the Federal Republic was integrated into the Western alliance, the quicker the formalization of an at least nominal East German sovereignty proceeded, very much against West German intentions and interests.

This, of course, raises the well-known question: Did Adenauer *et alii* deliberately sabotage a possible German reunification based on Soviet offers of negotiations in 1952 and later in 1955, by pursuing their policies of *Alles oder Nichts*, in order to save their political hegemony? As a direct answer to this would demand not only incomparably more knowledge of German history than we command, but even introspection and illumination in certain dark historic spots, we would rather try to answer a broader question: Could these Soviet offers represent an *objective possibility* for German reunification? We believe that the Soviet offer certainly did not mean such a possibility in 1952, though it could have meant an opening in 1955, when the initiative was in the hands of the United States rather than in West German diplomacy. As to the first offer, all available historical evidence refutes unequivocally any serious and honest intention on Stalin's part to let Germany reunite itself even on a Finlandized basis: he could only lose considerably and gain nothing. Given Soviet economic conditions right after the war, a unified and even Finlandized Germany had to loom as an economic giant over the USSR, boosting Western rather than Eastern economies. Although the Western nuclear monopoly had disappeared, there was no telling when the West could have won over the whole of Germany, once the Soviets allowed East Germany to slip from their grip, leaving them only the option of war, should they wish to rectify a disadvantageous strategic situation. At that time, the Gaullist option was yet to emerge; a German-Russian relationship that was too close could only forge much closer ties between the United States and the rest of Western Europe. All this is a strong refutation of the genuine character of Stalin's offer. Much more likely, it was an attempt to decelerate West German integration into the West.

The situation changed, however, after Stalin's death. A mysterious document, published by *Der Spiegel* in 1978, entitled the "Manifesto of the Union of Democratic Communists in the GDR" saw the situation in the GDR as follows: "All power struggles in the Political Bureau—Ackermann, Zaisser, Herrnstadt, Oelssner, Schirdewan, Ulbricht against Honecker—were connected with the national problem."* Such a comment may well be an accurate assessment of views on the national question in the GDR; indeed, it takes on particular significance because Zaisser, the minister of interior, was closely linked with Beria and was eliminated from the leadership, and later from the party, after the arrest and execution of his Moscow protector. Rumors have been circulating ever since to the effect that Beria wanted "to sell out the GDR," in other words, that the option which under Stalin had been a mere propaganda exercise had become a serious, if not necessarily honest, bargaining position. A crucial piece of irrefutable evidence, which had hitherto escaped the attention of German historians, has now been published, verifying that Beria did want to initiate a deal that included the possible abandonment of the GDR to the West for an undisclosed price (an offer which more than likely never reached the State Department). The evidence stems from the then third most senior official of the Italian Communist Party, Pietro Secchia.† Given what communist politics have always been, the outcome of the Beria option is not an argument against but rather one for the genuine character of the 1955 Soviet offer about Germany. Indeed, his colleagues had murdered Beria two years earlier (as he would have murdered them) using, among others, the pretext of his "treason" in the German question as a justification, but they might have made a mental note of the remarkable idea and put it to use, as a "Marxist-Leninist approach to a complex problem," in 1955. In our book on the Hungarian Revolution‡ we have argued that the first post-Stalin leadership, being in throes of infighting and rebellions affecting almost the whole of the empire, at least could have been amenable to early openings to détente. Therefore, that this historic opportunity was not used is, to a very great extent, a Western

*Brandt and Ammon, eds., *Die Linke und die nationale Frage*, p. 343.

†The detailed story of Secchia's evidence is recounted in F. Fehér and A. Heller, *Eastern Europe under the Shadow of a New Rapallo*, Study No. 6, "Crisis in Soviet-Type Systems," directed by Zdeněk Mlynář (Munich, 1984).

‡F. Fehér and A. Heller, *Hungary, 1956 Revisited* (London: George Allen and Unwin, 1983).

(primarily American but perhaps also West German) responsibility.

We have seen how the Adenauer option had unwittingly promoted the consolidation of the East German apparatus in the form of a state with nominal sovereignty (an apparatus which sees no short-term chance of seizing power throughout the whole of Germany and is therefore at least as insensitive to German reunification as the Left assumes the Adenauer leadership had been). A further, and less obvious, consequence of the Adenauer option has been formulated by Peter Brückner in a way that is characteristic of the conception of wider trends on the West German Left. One of the important opposition forces, namely, the communists, Brückner remarks, exists in Germany *in the form of a state*. And this ingenuous formulation expresses one of the most fatal self-delusions of the West German Left. The point is, of course, that the GDR is not a political party on the left of the West German *diapazon*, but an oppressive state beyond the alternatives of "right" and "left." Finally, there is constantly a measure of ambivalence discernible in West German attitudes, on both the Right and the Left, toward East Germany, even when its existence as a state has been accepted. The SPD had fought for a long time for the recognition of the GDR as a sovereign state, but Egon Bahr, the main expert on intra-German, and more recently on defense, matters within the SPD argued in 1963 that the correct method of proceeding in the German problem is as follows: "The preconditions for reunification can only be created with the Soviet Union. They are not to be attained in East Berlin."* This is not just a graphic representation of an authentic social democratic conception of the "sovereign state" which they had otherwise intended to recognize, but also that of a traditional type of German politicking: a politics always conducted "from above," always in the form of the sublime (and invariably unrealistic) designs of so many Marquis Posas, always with demonstrable hostility to social movements. The present, uncritical collapse of the German social democracy before certain deeply problematic tendencies of the antinuclear movement, and what will follow from it in terms of political consequences, is a justly deserved historical punishment for their haughty superiority against movements over a period of twenty years.

The German constellation underwent a gradual but radical change from the early sixties onward, the most visible political result of which was the end of the political hegemony of the CDU-CSU and the gradual

---

*Brandt and Ammon, eds., *Die Linke und die nationale Frage*, p. 235.

conquest of power (in alliance with the Free Democrats) by the SPD. The causes of the change can be summed up in a laconic way. First, the Adenauer option had been fully implemented: the Federal Republic not only had been integrated into the Western alliance as an (almost entirely) sovereign state but it had also become its main "continental" power. As this feat completed the historical task Adenauer had vowed to achieve, and as it had unwittingly accelerated the emergence of the GDR, in itself a symbolic sign of the impossibility of German reunification on Adenauer's premises, there was indeed no historical mission the Christian Union could have further fulfilled. Second, whereas the German *Wirtschaftswunder*, which was a miracle indeed in the sense that it transformed an almost destroyed Germany into the wealthiest nation of the European West, was a kind of "consolation prize" for an irretrievably lost national unity and hurt national pride, there emerged certain structural social problems that a self-consciously procapitalist, conservative government could not change. The time was ripe for a change, even if later the change brought more disillusionment than fulfillment. Third, after the Berlin crisis, the cold war started to "slacken" and give way (in the form of confidential communications between Khrushchev and Kennedy) to what later became Kissinger's strategic option. The Vietnam war rechanneled tensions away from Europe to Asia, so that a central argument of the Christian Union, that their unyielding vigor alone could protect the new state, could no longer captivate the majority of an electorate whose needs and political priorities were altering. Finally, social democracy, too, underwent a number of changes under the impact of a new generation of leaders. On the one hand, the social democrats gave up Schumacher's nationalism and accepted the integration of West Germany into the Western alliance, while on the other hand, they tamed (in Bad Godesberg) their socialist ambitions. They gradually became sensitive to a new opening, which later gained notoriety under the name of *Neue Ostpolitik*, and which, in objective terms, completed Adenauer's mission. While the conservative chancellor reassured the West that the Federal Republic was a German nation-state and not a nucleus of a German Reich, the social democratic chancellor emphasized that a Germany led by his party had abandoned forever any idea of going beyond the Oder-Neisse line. In this sense, Adenauer and Brandt are not so much political enemies as complementary figures of a postwar German history.

The real content of an impending and important political change is spelled out by Rudolf Augstein. This is how he saw *Neue Ostpolitik*, long before *Der Spiegel* became a mouthpiece for Brandt's policy:

Supposing we had, despite everything, a government capable of action, what could it do? As a first task, it ought to perceive that a threat of war in Europe does not arise from itself, not because of the devilishness of the godless Bolsheviks, but above all, because of the intricacies of the German question. The present borderlines must be recognized, in order for Poland and Czechoslovakia to proceed further toward independence. The pressure of German revisionism, I deliberately use here an originally communist vocabulary, has to be eliminated from the whole of Eastern Europe. Friendly relations of all kind, obviously diplomatic relations as well, should be cultivated with governments of the former satellite countries. This in itself would be a lot. Secondly, one must not sabotage, ridicule or countermand the operations of both world powers for they cannot withdraw from the center of Europe without endangering the European balance, and as such their presence should be constructively supported. Without a nuclear-free zone in Central Europe, without a disentanglement of the military blocks, without armament control and the reduction of troops in a limited area . . . there is no chance for an inner-German rapprochement, no chance for the re-Europeanization of the former satellite countries. An absolute reconsideration is necessary here, and in a very un-German fashion, namely, reconsideration as nonwishful thinking. If the Soviets left just Poland, Hungary and Germany, progress would be guaranteed. If the Americans left the continent, De Gaulle, or whoever steps in his boots, would be obliged to be satisfied. Clearly, without the USA as a guarantor of a European settlement there could be none. Just as France and Sweden guaranteed the Treaty of Westphalia, so too the USA and the USSR, whether we like it or not, are the guarantors of all systems in present Europe. Thirdly, and finally, the GDR, with all the false pretenses conveyed in her name, should be brought, through collaboration, through manifold economic merger, even through economic aid, to a higher level. Whether its government is a German government is a question which, for very good reasons, is at least open to doubt; that it is a *de facto* authority, even a government, is not. . . . It is in our interests that the GDR authorities should become a government without inverted commas, a more independent, more self-conscious body. Our interest is that the GDR government should be more German, a German government. . . . Be it communist or whatever else you wish to call it, this should not bother us.*

The balance of the *Ostpolitik* can be summed up in the following terms. First, the new leaders of Germany, who made it public knowledge that they felt shame and remorse for the horrendous deeds com-

*Brandt and Ammon, eds., *Die Linke und die nationale Frage*, pp. 244–45. The text was published in *Der Spiegel* in 1965.

mitted in the name of Germany and by German hands, who in a way had taken the responsibility upon themselves, although often they had been victims or targets of persecution themselves, fulfilled a historical duty for their nation and for the rest of humanity, without which there could never be reconciliation. It should be added that this duty has never been done in a sincere way by the politicians of the conservative parties. Second, and not independently of the aforementioned, *Neue Ostpolitik* has defused the tension from the Soviet-German relationship, not only at an official level, but also at the social base. The "German revanchist" scarecrow could be brought into play during the Dubček period by Soviet propaganda, but no longer. These two factors were considerable contributions to defusing the cold war in general. Third, the process of "merging" the GDR economy with the West German, making Honecker's Germany a silent partner in the European Economic Community through West German channels, was also an organic part of *Ostpolitik*. If this opening is assessed from an exclusively nationalistic point of view, it was, of course, successful in the sense that the GDR, promoted by both the Soviets and the Federal Republic, has attained the best standard of living within the Eastern block and thus could further pass certain economic burdens to the West German taxpayers. If this process is evaluated from the value of freedom (democracy), however, it was a total flop. No serious liberalization of the GDR has been achieved, or demanded, other than some increase in family reunions. Honecker's "workers and peasants republic," about which the West German Left regularly lapses into delusion, has remained, together with Turkey and Albania, the most repressive country of Europe since the overthrow or gradual demolition of dictatorships in Portugal, Greece, and Spain (if, of course, the Soviet Union is not included in this cluster). Fourth, here too the basic ideological self-delusion of the Brandt-Schmidt era, "piecemeal engineering," showed its Janus face. The new slogan that came into vogue with the Bad Godesberg revision of the Marxist tradition was part of a package deal: accepting a hotchpotch of American sociology of "industrial society" and abandoning any idea of a radical socialist strategy, Marxist or non-Marxist. What was of course covered over by the surface optimism of the program of "piecemeal engineering" is *the actual postponement of all genuine attempts at German reunification ad calendas Graeca*. This was even more characteristic of the Schmidt period, where the chancellor could say as the optimum of his Germany policy that the problem "has remained open." The SPD, which had abandoned Schumacher's nationalism but which had come to power with a criticism of the cold war romanticism and with the promise that the realism of its piecemeal engineering would produce results that could not be produced under CDU-CSU illusionism, achieved exactly the same as its predecessors: no progress at all.

What are, if any, the abstract-logical chances of a German reunification in such a situation, seen from a Western as well as an Eastern point of view? For reasons that will become immediately clear, it is easier to start with the Eastern perspective. For the GDR, only logically speaking, the Beria option has always existed, that is, being sold out to the West by the Soviet masters in return for some kind of a global bargain between the superpowers. If we mean by "GDR" the ruling apparatus and not the populace (for the latter it would be, of course, liberation), this has, in our firm view, never been an option seriously considered by any faction of the apparatus. The Beria option would have forced the East German nomenklatura to take one of two courses: either radically to mend their ways to a point where they could become what they had never been or to reduce themselves to political insignificance from their present, all-powerful position. Further, again logically speaking, there is the chance of "Yugoslavization," that is, a considerable degree of inner liberalization together with an increasing measure of relative independence from the Soviet Union. This option is now seen as a guaranteed panacea in some quarters of the West German political scene. It would not be fair to say that it is merely a logical possibility, but its implementation nevertheless would depend on entirely different factors from the ones suggested by West German analysts. In short, it cannot come *before* some form of reunification is implemented, only *after* a confederation in which the formal hold of the USSR (which makes an intervention against potential East German "Titoists" even "legitimate") over the GDR has been loosened. Even after a confederation, however, this would be a much less likely outcome of events given the nature of East German communism. Indeed, confederation with the GDR would undoubtedly entail risks and exact a heavy price: the "Finlandization" of West Germany would be a better description of the likely outcome of confederation.

Third, as a hypothetical possibility, there could emerge a "gradual unification," a "piecemeal merger" of the two new German states. Willy Brandt and the SPD nurtured some such hopes; their incomparably more realistic GDR counterparts, however, never have. Willy Stoph made this very clear during the 1970 Erfurt meeting of the delegations of the two German states: "In fact, the two sovereign states, the GDR and the FRG, do not lend themselves to unification because contradicting social systems cannot be unified."\* For the ruling apparatus, unification would simply be a voluntary acceptance of the first version, the "Beria option," and here we are dealing with anything but fools.

Fourth, finally, the GDR has always recommended a single solution: *confederation*. This would provide a symbolic "cultural" satisfaction for the Western part, and several invaluable advantages for the East German apparatus. The single Western satisfaction would be *cultural-spiritual* unity at the price of self-Finlandization of the whole of Germany, which of course automatically means a return to one of the worst traditions of the German culture: a heightened patriotism without *political self-awareness*. For on the terms of self-Finlandization neither the critique of the East German part of Germany nor a genuinely (democratic) Western radicalism would be conceivable. It is easy, however, to enumerate the Eastern advantages. It would be a tremendous political victory for an oppressive apparatus, an actual confirmation for the most cynical of East German slogans, "*Wer mit der Sowjet-Union ist, ist mit dem Sieger.*" Further, it is easy to conceive the *economic* advantages of such a confederation for a highly industrialized country (the GDR is actually the fifth industrial power of Europe) that suffers, because of its social system, from incurable diseases as far as economic-purposive rationality is concerned. Politically, the terms of a self-Finlandization of the whole of Germany (the only price at which it is at least theoretically conceivable that the Russian apparatus should agree to a confederation) would allow the East German apparatus to take any course it deemed fit. The most likely one would be to carry on business in as harsh a manner as usual, with one exception—that it would have to make (and is in fact now already making) concessions concerning travel of citizens within Germany. At the same time, it would become a bridgehead for a later submission of the whole of Germany to the needs of Soviet expansionism.

As far as the Western strategy of reunification is concerned, there have always been two options, hardly spelled out publicly but inevitably included in the unrealistic alternative of *Alles oder Nichts*. The first was an American victory over the Soviet Union, the second a new Russian revolution or a collapse of the USSR in some unforeseen way

---

\*Brandt and Ammon, eds., *Die Linke und die nationale Frage*, p. 310.

(in which case reunification would be a matter of course). The first has become in the meantime a physical impossibility in the sense that it entails an all-out nuclear war, which has no winners, and after which the survivors would have somewhat more urgent tasks than the reunification of the two parts of Germany. The second is neither a theoretical nor a physical impossibility, but it is a political nonoption because it is an alternative in the direction of which no German political activity can be pursued. Therefore it is a pious or impious wish. A third possibility existed (but no longer does) in the form of the "Beria option." While it would have been suicide for the East German apparatus, it would have been, up until the early sixties, a realistic alternative for the West.

A fourth theoretical option is a special *German-Russian bargain*, a simple rehash of the 1922 Rapallo treaty for which, however, the preconditions are absent and not likely ever to arise again. Rapallo was the agreement of two almost equally weak big powers which mutually needed one another and which could offer several advantages to each other. Now West Germany and the USSR are equally strong, but in different ways. The USSR is the leading military power of the world, with an East European empire of satellites bordering on West Germany and an increasing number of bases all over the world. At the same time, its economy has remained, despite industrial growth, perpetually ailing, and in principle it would need heavy and long-term West German investments. However, the inequality in the first aspect is so enormous (and without a West German nuclear self-armament, which is a virtual impossibility, such inequality could not be eliminated) and the risks of the second course are so complex and unpredictable for West German capital that these factors do not allow for a simple repeat performance of Rapallo 1922. Further, there is the theoretical possibility of renouncing, once and for all, the idea of German reunification in exchange for being part of the West. The German need for reunification is so strong, however, that no elected German government can afford such a formal gesture. (Even the nonelected German government publicly offers a historical and distant outlet for such hopes.)

What finally remains is the exact opposite of the third alternative: the *self-Finlandization* of West Germany, which used to be regarded as nonsense, a nonoption, but is no longer. It has become an actual, genuine option on the agenda. Its actual form can only be confederation, with the East German apparatus retaining its power over the populace and its total inner independence, its precondition the West German abandonment of NATO and practical German disarmament.

Whatever the West German illusions concerning a ''reunification on federal-republican terms'' might be, it can only happen in the Finnish way: making German sovereignty *formally dependent* on Soviet approval of major affairs, at least, for the time being, as far as external affairs are concerned. *This is the task on the agenda of the New Rapallo.* This alternative can be called condescendingly by the experts of West German politics a mere nightmare of a feverish dissident fantasy, but in fact it has turned into a genuine option.

What made such an unlikely option, once virtually inconceivable, a genuine alternative in less than a decade? The first cause is a political and economic transformation of the West. The West *now* without West Germany would be powerless in Europe, therefore Germany (i.e., the Federal Republic) no longer has any reason for waiting for ''the West'' to do something for or against the Germans. If anyone, the Germans, being almost identical with ''the West,'' can do something for themselves.

Secondly, between the Vietnam War and the Reagan period, *American hegemony collapsed.* Germans, whatever their politics, have always questioned whether America once had a magic formula for the German dilemma, as well as the intention to put it to use. Today this is no longer a question. The American administrations no longer have either the power or the professed intention to make a single serious step toward German reunification. For Americans, the German question is solved as best as it can be. However, this is certainly not the German view.

Three additional factors have to be added to this constellation. Despite an extremely competent ''crisis management'' (which is the best one could say of the Schmidt era), the curve of West German prosperity simply had to start to decline at a certain point, bringing with it the disappearance of the German ''consolation prize'' for a lost national unity and curtailed sovereignty. Further, the events from Czechoslovakia 1968 to Poland 1981 taught the important lesson (the morally and politically worst conclusions of which have been internalized in West Germany on the Left and the liberal Center) that the period of Khrushchevite reformism, always a dubious concept for Germans, was over, and that the USSR no longer sought to attract anyone by its ''human face''; it intends to command respect, fear, and obedience instead. Third, with the advent of the Reagan administration, the West has a powerful government that is *the least sensitive* since the French governments of the 1920s to German grievances. Reagan personally, and members of his administration collectively, committed all the possible mistakes concerning Germany (and Western Europe in general). Part of this policy has, of course, been structural for American capitalism: they have passed on the costs of a very limited and moderate American recovery to Western Europe. Another part was blundering, pure and simple.

All this resulted in what *Der Spiegel* called the "uprising against the missiles," and what has been termed by Karl Kaiser "national in the guise of antinuclear."* The term "uprising" is not simply journalistic sensationalism. In fact, behind the antimissile movement there is a movement against the Yalta-Potsdam system, the thrust of which comes from the "romantic Center" and the Left but which is increasingly spreading throughout Germany. In addition, it is far from accidental that this has been provoked by the missile issue. Of course, theorists of the antinuclear cause will argue that, indeed, the deployment of the Pershing and Cruise missiles is no mere accident but simply the last step in the concatenation of dangerous, irresponsible American acts. Therefore, in their view, the antimissile issue must be understood not in German national but rather in a global strategic and humanitarian context. One can state on the basis of the Brandt and Ammon collection of documents, however, that *the warehousing of missiles has always had a national importance* for all Germans who did not accept the Adenauer option as final. In other words, all antinuclear forces commenced their campaign, wittingly or unwittingly, at a point that both West and East regard as the symbolic, though real, obstacle to German reunification. The mainstream of the movement, whatever the original intention of those having joined it, is not so concerned about missiles but about German reunification. The latter is, let us repeat, a perfectly legitimate, even just cause; the question is, however (as always about instances of national unification), *in what ways and at what price it is going to be actualized.* Our criticism here will be grounded in more than a hundred years of socialist, democratic, and liberal traditions, which, to remain with the German example, strongly supported German unity *in abstracto* but, equally strongly, condemned the particular Bismarckian form in which it had been implemented.

The development toward a New Rapallo promises to be far from auspicious. The terms of such an agreement could only be such as to support a modification, with or without a formal peace treaty, of the Yalta-Potsdam agreement to the detriment of the West, in favor of the

*"National im anti-nuklearen Gewande (Egon Bahr und die Rückkehr zur sicherheitspolitischen Nationalstaatsidee)," *Die Zeit*, April 6, 1984.

USSR. A "neutralized" Germany that is hostile to the West, that exists under the foreign policy tutelage of the Soviet Union, and, with its tremendous technology and financial resources, that helps the Soviet regimes to allay their economic problems without any liberalization of their brutal inner system of oppression, thereby lending indirect support (ironically, through the success of an antinuclear peace movement) to the Soviet war machine, would be, after Hitler's victory or Stalin's immediate seizure of Western Europe, the worst possible conclusion of World War Two. And let us have no illusions: if it comes to a New Rapallo, these will be its terms, and its results.

Why is such a threat realistic? First, because of the increasing fragmentation of the Western alliance, due to a number of structural reasons. Second, because of the importance of certain "background factors," such as the weakening of American supremacy, but most importantly because of the dominant trends within the only potential subject that can conclude such an agreement, the German social democracy. One can almost see the condescending response of the "experts" to this. German social democracy, they would argue, will never turn against the Western alliance. Just recently, when it rejected the deployment of the new missiles, it renewed its commitment to the Western alliance. However, apart from the fact that in politics there is no such word as "never," apart from the fact that in 1978 all authoritative spokespersons of the British Labour Party would have denied as "enemy slander" the idea that they would ever embrace the unilateralist position that became official party policy within two years, there is more direct evidence supporting our thesis. Kaiser, in his article mentioned previously, terms the position of Bahr on security matters an (illusory) "return to the position of the nation-state which is irreconcilable with the idea of the alliance" (an accusation which Bahr could virtually not answer), a kind of German Gaullism that is lacking in the necessary preconditions of De Gaulle's policy. And Egon Bahr has been for twenty years somewhat more than the representative of idiosyncratic ideas in the SPD. In fact, the internal dynamics of the SPD pushes the party, as far as we can see, toward unilateralism which in the German case is identical with the neutralization of West Germany and the abandonment of the alliance.

This internal dynamics is well established in the deep contradictions of the party itself. On the one hand, the electoral defeat robbed the party of the only halo it had carried for a decade: the superior atmosphere of a *competent* pragmatism triumphant over "simplistic" social radicalism. German social democracy has failed in the only capacity in which it had seemed to be superior and competent, without becoming socially radical again in any genuine sense of the word. Therefore the SPD embraced nationalism, in the wake of romantic Centrists and national Bolsheviks whose undeniable merit was to declare war on the defeatist slogan of *Finis Germaniae*, who made public their "will to nation." But this nationalism, which commenced its deplorable career with the actual betrayal of Poland in 1981,* can only lead to a New Rapallo, the terms of which will facilitate an anti-Western conclusion to World War Two.

Could a New Rapallo, under the terms we delineated above, guide the German nation out of the antinomies it set for itself when it miscarried the anti-Hitler revolution? Our answer is unhesitatingly in the negative. A New Rapallo, if it achieves at least the symbol of unity—confederation—will once again bring the German nation to the crossroad where freedom and national idea meet to part ways for a very long, although not the first, time. A confederation could by no means alleviate the burdens of the Eastern (or "Middle") part of Germany, excepting only the admittedly crucial question of personal contacts between Germans. The inner system of oppression is not likely to be liberalized, and it certainly will not disappear. At the very best, West Germans would be able to keep their conservative-liberal state, which they call, rather appropriately, *Obrigkeitsstaat*. The latter could even become worse because of a possible new McCarthyism that would work against both Leftist and Rightist critics of the nationalist consensus that calls into being the New Rapallo. At any rate, it would certainly not provide social space for socialism as radical democracy. Germans of all colors now complain about their restricted sovereignty, and even

*The word "betrayal" has a dubious status in politics after sixty years of demagogic communist propaganda against social democrats. Nonetheless, we use it deliberately, for we think that German social democracy has never had, since the worst moments under Scheidemann and Noske, darker days morally than the ones in which Schmidt and Honecker together "felt regret" over what "had to happen" in Poland, in which Brandt in the name of the Second International toned down the protest to such a degree that the socialists of the Latin countries had to state publicly that the president of the Second International did not speak in their name. We all know what the moral justification is in such cases: we Germans have committed enough against Russians to remain silent, or at least subdued, when it is their turn. However, in the Polish case this is a strange, in short, a hypocritical argument. As to the rest of the West German Left, see Sigrid Meuschel's article, "Neo-nationalism and the West German Peace Movement's Reaction to the Polish Military Coup," *Telos* 56 (Summer 1983).

if the statements often seem to be excessive, sometimes inauthentic, the fact remains. In the wake of a New Rapallo, as a result of self-Finlandization, they would learn what it means to have a reduced national sovereignty *à la Sovietique*. And with all this, we have not even mentioned the possibility, obviously not imminent, of attempts at Sovietizing the whole of Germany, for which the confederation would at least provide a bridgehead.

The detailed analysis of the internal German situation in a chapter dealing with Soviet strategy is important because it is only on this basis that we can understand the main strategic line of Soviet expansionism in Europe. The Soviet Union combines the policy of making open threats (referring, of course, to its vulnerable position) with suggesting (and perhaps secretly making) offers of a way out of the reunification impasse. While it sometimes commits mistakes (such as the mass arrests of independent peace activists in East Germany in the aftermath of the Bundestag's decision to deploy the Pershing missiles, an act which provoked protest even from Petra Kelly), it is not likely to repeat such mistakes. It will obviously wait either until the CDU-CSU regime is voted out of office in a new election and a (then) overtly unilateralist SPD returns to power or until this trend spills over to part of the Right and a national consensus emerges concerning the abandonment of the Western alliance. This would be the historical moment to make a fundamentally new offer for a kind of German reunification. Stalin's successors would make a strong contribution to the legitimization of their repressive rule, if they could come up with one at the right moment. There is no telling whether they will indeed have the historical lucidity adequate for their historical chance. Once, in the hour of despair in 1941, they were capable of doing so. Throwing overboard a policy of divisiveness, they preached and reached a relative national consensus (of course, with the background support of Hitler). The fact is that, adding to the general picture the British situation, where the open crisis of the alliance is only postponed by the renewed Tory electoral victory, a disaster for the country socially and economically, but where the Soviets have no particular move to make, it suffices to wait and see. The Soviets have never had in forty years such historical openings as these. All the above can be legitimately called ''armchair strategic thinking''; in many ways it is. Everyone who contemplates a political constellation, however, must project its imaginable implications, and, as we have learned from Aristotle, there is no firm knowledge concerning the future, only opinion.

Is the peace, or antinuclear, movement a vehicle of Soviet expansionism? This question is generally inconsiderately answered in the analyses of liberals who understand the character but not the social causes of the movement; it is answered mostly in the form of an "agent theory."* The "agent theory" has, of course, a considerable amount of undeniable evidence supporting it. If one only thinks of West Germany (where one of Brandt's confidants, Günter Guillaume, was an East German intelligence service officer) or of Great Britain, where from Kim Philby to Sir Anthony Blunt a whole cluster of prominent intellectuals and highly placed public servants worked for the KGB and its predecessors, it is obvious from where a certain kind of dogged "spiritual unilateralism" comes. It would also be childish to assume that the KGB, which has a wide network everywhere, would not infiltrate this particular and extremely important movement, which, according to its very structure, has no precautionary measures, no screening system, where questions about one's past, even about one's present political position, are not asked for reasons of principle. It is also well known that the movement is teeming with notoriously pro-Soviet organizations which have consistently defended each and every act of internal and external Soviet oppression, such as the West German Communist Party (DKP), as well as individual activists of the same persuasion. In their case, there is no need even to mention intelligence organizations: they work for Soviet interests out of conviction (and for some benefits).

Despite all this, we find the "agent theory" totally misconceived, for a number of reasons. It has, above all, an inescapable cold war connotation. Hunting agents can only mean one thing: the denunciation to secret services (which are themselves screening the field) of people who either are or are not on the Soviet payroll and the demand for their harrassment by the force of public opinion. This is incompatible with democratic principles, as well as counterproductive: it will produce martyrs for a movement that is inclined to melodramatics. Further, the socially relevant question is why people lend credence to activists and views that ten years ago they would have dismissed with an ironical smile. Agent hunting can therefore never reach its proper goal: the transformation of the present stage and level of discourse in the anti-

---

*While the word "agent" is not used, the analysis nonetheless points in the direction of the "agent theory" in A. Chalfont's article, to mention only one extremely well-informed example.

nuclear movement. The latter itself lives in an atmosphere of similar (only differently located) suspicion of agents. If one agent theory confronts another, communication will break down altogether, and polemics will turn into a shouting match.

The Soviet leadership has scored one decisive victory that is more important than any number of agents: *they dominate the discourse in the antinuclear movement*. This statement is not equivalent to the assertion that those using functionally pro-Soviet arguments (and this is the situation with the majority of the leaders of opinion in the movement) are pro-Soviet in their sentiments or political commitments. It means that Soviet expansionism, which, together with the deepening inner crisis of the Western alliance, determines increasingly the political and intellectual situation in Western Europe—the kind of questions that are asked, the kind of answers that are given, and the kind of alternatives that are formulated in the movement. We are firmly convinced that almost invariably the wrong questions are asked, the wrong answers are given, and false alternatives are formulated. But once the intellectual starting point has been dominated and distorted, no agents are needed to do the brainwashing in order to arrive at invariably wrong conclusions. Achieving this is a surprising intellectual feat for a leading stratum that, taking into account several crucial aspects of their performance and especially the ''culture'' they generate and tolerate, is regarded as a ''bunch of dumb apparatchiks.'' This condescending attitude, however, harbors an underestimation of Leninism as a technology of power, its flexible capability of translating often very complex issues into the simple language of domination.

Which are the false premises and the wrong alternatives? In the main, there are two basic tenets, irreconcilably contradicting one another, but nonetheless regularly used simultaneously and by the same discussants in the antinuclear movement. One premise is that the Soviet Union is weak and threatened by a bellicose United States. This premise suggests an uncritical, self-hypnotic anti-Americanism in the movement which mixes good and bad in American policy without analysis, a hate of the ''East European troublemakers'' (Sigrid Meuschel's courageous article showed what contemptible depths this attitude has reached on the West German Left). The second premise is ''better Red than dead.'' If one is ready simply to understand what the maxim means at all (this is not often the case), one will understand that the only possible meaning is that the Soviet Union is strong, stronger than, or at least as strong as, the West. (Faithful to our methodology, we are not going to make any attempt to determine questions of military superiority between East and West.) It is at least strong enough to destroy us. Let us embrace the Soviet regime, therefore, in order to survive if need be. The second premise is, of course, logically irreconcilable with the first, but *both* must be, and indeed are, present in the antinuclear argument. The first component shows that the Soviet Union is a non-aggressive power on the defensive against an aggressive West and therefore carries no moral responsibility for whatever is happening; the second instills salutary fear of the Soviet military might and suggests the instinctive betrayal of all rebellions against Soviet oppression, which can only create danger. From this, the *permanent false alternative of the antinuclear discourse* inevitably follows. It is the alternative of life *or* freedom, a choice between the two branches of which no good decision is possible in an era of the universalistic values of modernity.

Is the antinuclear movement, then, a vehicle of Soviet expansionism? The movement emerged overwhelmingly from the indigenous problems of the West. In articulating these problems, it is a legitimate and autonomous movement of the West with wide social relevance and a contradictory potential that still can lead toward certain emancipatory results, although in our view it now has a stronger affinity for a nonemancipatory outcome. As long as the discourse is dominated by false premises and alternatives determined by Soviet expansionism, however, the movement is, without agents and despite the intentions of the majority of its participants, indeed a potential vehicle of this expansionism.

# IV.  The Antinuclear Movement

The main question about the antinuclear movement, which cannot be answered in terms of a rigidly liberal theory (ignorant of, or impervious to, the structural crisis of the West) and concerning which the movement itself is not willing to attain lucid self-awareness, is this: Why has the movement emerged at this time, in so many countries and in such a concerted way? The antinuclear theorist will simply answer that the increased danger of a confrontation has heightened (due to the Reagan administration, the technological propensities of the new missiles, and, more balanced observers would say, the escalation of the armaments race on both sides); therefore, global nuclear war is imminent. We have rejected this prediction and therefore cannot accept the latter explanation as an adequate account of the recent growth of the movement.* There is no evolutionist answer either. Without being historians of the antinuclear movement, we can state the following fundamental facts. Up until the end of the 1950s, the only international *organization* with an antinuclear profile was the World Peace Council, a Soviet front organization that still exists but which has lost its impor-

---

*We have historical arguments as well. Public opinion in the West must have known at least since the late fifties that we are living in a state of "overkill." In fact, the Kennedy administration, which on the one hand pushed through an updating of the American nuclear arsenal similar in relative size to what is happening under Reagan but which on the other hand wanted to make test bans palatable to an American public still suffering the lingering final effects of the cold war, publicly and dramatically warned about the inherent danger of Doomsday. The clashes between the superpowers (from Korea to Berlin and from Cuba to Vietnam, in the form of direct confrontations or through proxies) were more frequent and obvious. Statesmen and military commanders improvised publicly, or almost publicly, with the idea of (preemptive, limited, tactical, retaliatory) nuclear strikes, an idea which then was still not excommunicated from the public vocabulary. Nonetheless, in the whole period there were no movements in evidence. Certainly, therefore, there must be some other explanation.

tance, even for Soviet leaders, with the emergence of autonomous antinuclear movements. Its position was very simple: Western nuclear weapons are a threat, Soviet nuclear armaments are a guarantee of world peace. This simple logic is still upheld in the official peace organizations of the Eastern bloc. In Great Britain the Campaign for the Nuclear Disarmament (CND) has held to a unilateralist position from its inception. As we all know, the accusations by the liberal and the Rightist press that Labour was unilateralist had been vehemently denied by Labour Party spokesmen and militants up until roughly 1978. Somewhat later the party accepted the CND program and has retained it, with interesting stubbornness, despite the fact that unilateralism, according to almost all observers, was the main reason for Labour's landslide defeat in the 1983 elections. In spite of our ignorance of antinuclear history, we are not entirely convinced by Chalfont's interpretation of CND as simply a communist Trojan horse. He may be more familiar with the facts than we are, and therefore he could be right: a then totally Stalinist British communism backed the movement in the 1950s without reservation. But even so, an additional explanation is needed to understand why it was only in Great Britain that a *movement* emerged in the fifties. Our hypothesis is that Bertrand Russell's personality and political transition from a cold warrior to an ardent enemy of the United States holds the key to this phenomenon. One must not necessarily accept I. L. Horowitz's marked aversion to the whole of Russell's work to share his view that it was an anti-American resentment and not a Leftist, or even consistently pacifist, conviction that led Russell in many of his public gestures. This resentment against ''American perfidy'' widely shared in Great Britain, and certainly not only on the Left, could have contributed to the CND becoming a movement, not just an insignificant front organization like many other ''national councils'' of the World Peace Council. At any rate, now we see an international network of groups, organizations, ideological and propaganda activities, a network of communication between them, indeed, almost an antinuclear culture. In addition, the fever has spread over countries that are either neutral (Sweden and, to a lesser extent, Austria and Switzerland) and are therefore not exposed to any alleged or real dangers related to nuclear armaments, or that are far removed from the European scene (Australia, New Zealand) and therefore do not directly confront the problems stemming from the deployment of missiles in Europe. This phenomenon is not explained by any theory, and it needs to be accounted for.

In our view, the recent worldwide growth of the antinuclear movement is not the result of any imminent danger of a global nuclear clash between the superpowers. *It is rather the powerful symbolic reaction of wide strata of Western society to three interrelated, crucial events of the last decade: the global economic depression* (which also means the erosion of several fundamental benefits and values of the Western way of life), *the end of global American hegemony,* and *the disappearance of all hopes of a "new world" or "reformed socialism."* It is this complex constellation to which the antinuclear movements react in a symbolic way, by articulating genuine issues but in terms of the misleading, albeit telling, conceptualization of a conflict between life and freedom. We believe that it is from this triple cause and the symbolic reaction to it that the merits and demerits of antinuclearism, its chances and limitations, its structures, its emancipatory potential, and the dangers inherent in it can be understood. Here, however, we owe the reader a conceptual clarification: What do we mean by "symbolic action"? Symbolic actions are such as targeted on an object that replaces for them the complexity of social problems that are not grasped and solved when we act on the object. Symbolic action is not an action of "false consciousness" if it is really representative. Moreover, it becomes symbolic action in an interrelationship between actor and observer in which the symbolic character of action will be exposed. Exposition means self-education of the observer. The observer declares the (symbolic) object or target of an action a "mere symbol" and suggests issues and objects behind it. But it is only in the actor's insistence on his or her own issue, in the manner, arguments, etc. of this insistence, that the real issues come to be revealed, or rather constituted. The symbolic action is reciprocal in character. Without dialogue there is no symbol, nor is there "issue behind the symbol." The relatively large number of symbolic actions in modernity is simply an indication of the complex character of modernity which cannot be grasped exhaustively by any action with either a consciously circumscribed objective or one deliberately targeted on a symbol. Symbolic action proper will always prove defective and, at the same time, illuminating in our approach to the complexity of modernity.

The worldwide depression is the longest, even if not the stormiest, in the history of capitalism.* The present is not only the longest crisis but

---

*This is, of course, an arguable statement. As even the crash-course student of modern economic history knows, unemployment in the United States eased considerably only with the advent of war, which meant a sudden upward turn in the armaments industry. Nonetheless, there is wisdom in the periodization of the crisis as taking place between 1929 and 1933 for, under the impact of a number of factors, the light at the end of the economic tunnel was already visible in 1933.

one that emerged under very peculiar circumstances. In the immediate postwar atmosphere of the Western world a consensus came about that seemed to be shared even by the opponents of capitalist economic and social organization. There were three, apparently unassailable, principles on which that consensus rested. First, both the Right and the Left shared the view that the West had been living a period of unprecedented technological revolution, which in itself guarantees an affluent society. Liberal and neo-Marxist theories alike departed from this combined conception of the affluent technological era, the only difference between the two conceptions being that liberalism regarded it as a blessing, while for the New Left ideology it was a curse, a factor paralyzing genuine radicalism. Second, friends and foes of Western capitalism alike believed that the latter could be scientifically regulated and protected from regularly recurring declines. The official adoption of Keynesian policies suggested a "scientific era," and only a few traditional Marxists remained adamant that all this was little more than a facade behind which new crises were fomenting. The dominant liberal historical-political theory accounted for the catastrophes of World War Two with the prewar elites' insufficient insight in social affairs. This criticism explicitly contained the self-assured promise: a constellation like that must not, and will not, repeat itself. Third, the welfare state (certain fundamental mechanisms that have been introduced in all leading industrial countries regardless of the nature of the political structure) was generally considered to be a guarantee of fundamental social and life security. Full employment seemed to be accepted as a human right; a spiral of constantly increasing real monetary incomes was more or less generally regarded as a natural course of events, something which was incumbent upon the state to deliver; and people began to look forward to a perhaps not too distant period in which education and health care would be free. Very low inflation rates, stable national currencies, at least in the key countries, and slow, almost "natural" price rises were important collateral features of this guaranteed security. When the depression set in, it was not just "hard times" that appeared again on the horizon. *It was indeed the end of a world that had seemed to be as good as its promises.* No wonder then that the major image that emerges out of it is the symbolic end of the world, nuclear holocaust.

This atmosphere of the coming "end of the world" (and not just the end of a period of the Western world) had two major, equally negative, atmospheric yields. The first is the transformation of a shallow, optimistic image of the future into the negative futurology of Doomsday, which in practical terms is identical with *the loss of the future of a whole world*. Beyond doubt, the image of the future in the era of an "economic miracle" was optimistic in a very shallow way, and it has produced its own typical pseudo-science: futurology. The simple trick of futurology consisted in a hypostatization of the existing trend. The present culture industry, with its dominant image of our day-to-day existence under the shadow of the mushroom cloud, exploits our cheap sentimentality for ourselves to the same extent as the propaganda of the affluent society exploited the cheapest version of our hedonistic expectations, with reversed emotional signs. A decade ago, future growth, security, affluence, harmony seemed to be endless and endlessly expanding. Now there is no growth, no affluence, no security, no harmony ahead of us, just nothing, or more precisely *nought*.* This is existential time indeed, but without the emphasis on freedom which was the dynamic spirit, and the great attraction, of Sartre's philosophy in an immediate postwar world. At the same time, and strangely enough, this is a masochistic universe. In a post–World War One atmosphere, Europe had reacted to the first cracks in a very thin wall of security with a flare-up of various necrophile social experiments. Now the Western world turns, in a very wide consensus, on the Left and on the Right, against its own principles, values, gods, and icons, sometimes paralyzed by the stronger, sometimes lured by the underdeveloped.

The second negative constituent of this "end of the world" atmosphere is that *fear becomes the major political socializing factor*. Of course, invoking Spinoza's or Goethe's Stoic Epicureanism, an ethics which demanded that normally socialized man should live without fear and hope, this never meant that certain social perspectives or taboos should not be "feared." Aristotle's famous and wise advice about the reasonable form of fear where people are aware of what is to be feared, under what circumstances, and to what extent, cannot be more relevant than in these days. It is precisely these necessary qualifications constitutive of a *reasonable* form of fear that are absent in the present atmosphere of Apocalypse that inundates our daily life.† It is an atmosphere that is truly necrophilic, based on a fantasy that is technological

---

*Speaking of this phenomenon, Glucksmann mentions, in our view correctly, "nihilism" and refers to Nietzsche as the father of this gesture of "embracing nought collectively." (By the way, this would explain the Nietzsche renaissance as well.) " 'Better will nought than will nothing'—Nietzsche said." "La nuova ideologia tedesca." Interview with Andre Glucksmann, *Mondoperaio* (Rome) 11 (November 1983), p. 128.

†Consistent and philosophically conscious theorists of the antinuclear move-

sphere that is truly necrophilic, based on a fantasy that is technological to pathologic excess, a daily reminder of Sarajevo at every minor juncture of a habitually turbulent world politics, a masochistic, symbolic, and imaginary-anticipative autopsy of the dead body of our civilization, the rhetoric and public (ironically, German) question of the excellent writer to his still living citizens: "When are we going to burn?" The skeleton, this time not in the cupboard but on constant public display, cannot socialize anyone else but the man of *angst*, a social actor who is preprogrammed to hysteria, passivity, and hostility to rational discourse. We shall later try to analyze the state and level of communication in the antinuclear movement. Here it will suffice to remark that the more than usual intolerance toward dissenting opinion in the movement follows naturally from an upbringing in this atmosphere of fear, even panic. In its sombre mood and obscure illumination the dissenting view is presented as the agent of Apocalypse.

The second major constituent of the present-day global constellation should be put in historical perspective. This cannot be performed in any better way than by quoting a succinct and deep presentation of Immanuel Wallerstein. He analyzes "the three instances in which one of the strong states achieved temporarily a period of relative dominance over the others—a relative dominance that we may call hegemony."

> The three instances are the hegemony of the United Provinces (Netherlands) in the mid-seventeenth century, that of Great Britain in the mid-nineteenth, and that of the United States in the mid-twentieth. In each case, hegemony came after the defeat of a military pretender to conquest (the Hapsburgs, France, Germany). Each hegemony was sealed by a "world war"—a massive, land-centered, highly destructive, thirty-year-long intermittent struggle involving all the major military powers of the time. These were respectively the Thirty Years' War of 1618-1648, the

---

ment try to provide the cult of fear (which they hitherto referred to as *angst* and regarded as alienation) with a "profound dimension" and a beneficial social function. F. Cerutti, who sees in the antinuclear movement a reemergence of a lost reason, writes the following: "The annual assembly of the German Evangelical Church was held in 1981, in the year of the birth of a new peace movement, in the sign of the biblical motto: *Fürchtet Euch!* (have fear!). A political philosophy that today would resume the theme of reason ought to relate it to this irrational force, by contributing to the paralyzation of *angst* and the mobilization of beneficial fear, to the reevocation of the shock of Hiroshima so easily dismissed." "Ragione, guerra, futuro," *Critica Marxista* (Rome, 1983), p. 61. Just the contrary, we would object to this recent pirouette of "dialectical reason." A political philosophy the overarching category of which is fear, beneficial or not, can only condition us to one of two extremes: desertion-capitulation or overaggressiveness.

Napoleonic Wars (1792–1815), and the twentieth-century conflicts between 1914 and 1945 which should properly be conceived as a single, long
"world war." It is to be noted that, in each case, the victor had been
primarily a maritime power prior to "world war," but had transformed
itself into a land power in order to win this war against a historically
strong land power which seemed to be trying to transform the world-
economy into a world-empire. The basis of the victory was not, however,
military. The primary reality was economic: the ability of accumulators of
capital located in the particular states to outcompete all others in all three
major economic spheres—agro-industrial production, commerce, and fi-
nance. . . . Each of these hegemonies was brief. Each came to an end
largely for economic reasons more than for politico-military reasons. In
each case, the temporary triple economic advantage came up against two
hard rocks of capitalist reality. First, the factors that made for greater
economic efficiency could always be copied by others—not by the truly
weak but those who had medium strength—and latecomers to any given
economic process tend to have the advantage of not having to amortize
older stock. Secondly, the hegemonic power had every interest in maintaining uninterrupted economic activity and therefore tended to buy labor
peace with internal redistribution. Over time, this led to reduced competi-
tiveness thereby ending hegemony. In addition, the conversion of the
hegemonic power to one with far-flung land and maritime military "re-
sponsibilities" involved a growing economic burden on the hegemonic
state, thus undoing its pre-"world war" low level expenditure on the
military.*

One could certainly list a number of technical objections to this bold
conception—for instance, was the Dutch hegemony politico-military as
well as economic? Does the factor of internal redistribution apply to the
United States to the same extent as it did to Great Britain? And,
obversely, did Great Britain truly suffer so seriously under the burdens
of a military budget accepted in exchange for world hegemony? But all
this is of secondary importance. Our major problem is rather that
Wallerstein's extremely original theory, strictly economic-reductionist
as always, cannot explain why it is reasonable to speak of an *American
responsibility* in the political climate created in the wake of world
hegemony. One cannot reasonably "criticize" almost automatic economic processes sociologically, politically, and morally; they simply
"have to happen" the way they happen. Further, according to our
theory, which regards the political organization of modernity not sim-

---

*Immanual Wallerstein, *Historical Capitalism* (London: Verso Editions, 1983),
pp. 58–60.

ply as a "superstructure" but as a separate logic or dynamic, we do not believe that an economic-reductionist view, with all the illuminating and novel insights it does provide, can account for the complexity of the present situation. Strictly economically speaking, three processes, each eroding the American world hegemony, have taken place relatively separately. The first is precisely the one mentioned by Wallerstein. The acceptance of the military budget burden that goes with a hegemonic position has proved to be too onerous even for the powerful American economy. Secondly, American administrations built up a skeleton of a global economy centered on the dollar and America's industrial superiority, which had too many unstable variables for its continued functioning (the unquestionable superiority and stability of the dominant currency, a practically unlimited field of investment and elastically expanding inner markets, no depression in the United States where the slightest turbulence of economic life would upset a whole global system). Such a multiplicity of optimum requirements could not be upheld for a long time, and indeed they were not. Thirdly, there was a deep inconsistency between the military-strategic and the economic-strategic thinking of the American power elite. In terms of the first, a rapid restoration and transcendence of the prewar economic level was needed on the part of the European and industrialized Asian allies, earlier friends and enemies alike. In terms of the latter, the unchallenged economic superiority of the United States had to be maintained for an indefinite period of time. When the first postulate had been realized, and had brought with it economic challengers—first of all, ironically, the two defeated powers, Germany and Japan—the American economy had to face new and unexpected problems which proved to be unmanageable for them. *The end of American hegemony*, and this is an important factor in the present-day "end of the world" atmosphere, acted with other factors to trigger a worldwide depression, which, in the form of the American budget deficit passed on to other nations through high interest rates and other channels, has struck the world as the "American plague." American politicians and citizens can argue that this is an absolutely ungenerous attitude given that America carries the main burdens for the defense of the Western world, which in its overwhelming majority has hitherto wanted to be defended, and also that this attitude is totally forgetful of the American postwar aid that helped these nations get on their feet. While this view is at least partly true, because of the syndrome we call *the American responsibility* this plea now carries a very diminished persuasive power.

Of what does the American responsibility consist? The United States appeared at the end of World War Two as the great democracy ushering in a new world era of democracy, and in fact it created the "free world," which is a combination of politically free states (some of which, Germany and Japan first of all, owe their political freedom directly to the United States) as well as political tyrannies in Latin America, Asia, and, to a lesser extent, Africa. The United States also relayed to the rest of the world the message that colonialism was doomed, and it was indeed instrumental in the collapse of colonial regimes (above all in the British colonies, something which has never been really forgiven in Great Britain, and not only on the political Right). At the same time, in Central America and in the cruel, strategically misconceived, and finally devastatingly unsuccessful Vietnam War, they introduced a system that Raymond Aron, a commentator sympathetic to the American political elite, has termed "imperial." It is not colonialism, but it is a form of economically and strategically motivated expansionism and domination that is morally scandalous and runs counter to the democratic principles the United States officially declares as its own. The United States has established a global economic and military system with the explicit purpose of ensuring worldwide democracy and global affluence, but this system (let us now focus on the military organization only) is run, under American "leadership," in a way that is increasingly unacceptable even for the staunchest ally. The executive prerogative of the American president over the nuclear weapons stationed in other countries factually delimits their sovereignty, and while the American leadership acknowledges the right of European presidents and prime ministers to veto an eventual use of nuclear weapons, they are not even ready to discuss the perfectly natural demand of the "double key." They demand allegiance but are not ready to let themselves be influenced in strategic decisions (in the case of the reactionary and stupid Grenada adventure, they did not even listen to Mrs. Thatcher). Their hypothetical strategies are conceived in terms of what is acceptable for Americans, which could be natural, but then it is also natural that Europeans feel a deep resentment against this attitude. (Chancellor Schmidt, another loyal supporter, and perhaps the most clever of them all, after his resignation addressed bitter reproaches to President Carter for terming weapons that can hypothetically result in the extinction of whole European nations "tactical" and, on that basis, not including them in the SALT II bargaining.) Americans—citizens, tourists, diplomats, statesmen, and businessmen alike—flooded the postwar world with signs of their feeling of superiority (which is, again, natural enough if we take into consideration what the United States achieved in the lifetime of two generations). This attitude, however, apart from generating an equally natural resentment against American patronization, has also been practically discredited by the inability of the American political elite really to understand the world they in fact administer.

There is a special problem with American culture the problematic character of which is regarded as part of "American responsibility." Of course, a certain kind of European criticism of American culture either is ridden by the ghosts of a defunct European superiority that still regards the new continent as its own appendage and apprentice or very simply follows in the footstep of Goebbels' "cultural criticism" (for instance, when *Konkret*, a West German magazine published by arch-Stalinists, stated that Beethoven's Fifth Symphony alone is worth more than the whole of American culture). The following dilemma, however, cannot be denied. American culture as an original phenomenon, in the form in which it has been distributed throughout the world, was the culture par excellence of "mass society": cinema as Hollywood, the modern city as a combination of skyscrapers and freeways, electronic music, decorative arts centered on industrial objects, the stereotyped American hotel from the North to the South Pole, the televised era and its universal images. For everyone who has been educated in a European, Moslem, Hindu, or Buddhist tradition, the moral and aesthetic weaknesses of this mass culture are self-evident, and therefore its *balanced* criticism is justified. The complexity of the situation, however, is such that there is an aspect in which the United States created a unique culture of (mostly local and municipal) democracy, civic virtues, a sense of legality and fairness, an appreciation of performance and achievement, and an insistence on certain democratic norms that is just as unparalleled in modernity as Athens was in the ancient world, but which simply cannot be standardized, packed, and distributed all over the world; it only functions, as a culture, on its native soil. Ignoring this aspect of American culture makes an otherwise legitimately vehement cultural criticism pretty one-sided. Further, the American hegemonic role has put a serious strain on American democracy itself, precisely in an aspect that was observed by Tocqueville. As Tocqueville correctly saw, in the American system of democracy there is always a tendency to become fundamentalist in the sense that, unlike in the liberal countries, there are trends (in the municipalities, in state legislation, in the press, in the so powerful public opinion, even if not necessarily at the level of federation) to formulate certain *substantive imperatives*, the observance or nonobservance of which makes someone acceptable or unacceptable, a true patriot or a traitor. The world hegemony brought with itself the unpleasant novelty (in the ominous period of McCarthyism) that such substantive imperatives appeared, and in a coercive form, on the level of the federal state, and for a moment they threatened to engulf American democracy as a whole. This trend, not accidentally, came to a halt. Therefore all hysterical demagoguery about an incipient or growing "fascism" in the United States (where no single democratic institution has been undermined, and some of them, for instance the supreme court, have become more powerful) is precisely this: demagoguery. It is important, however, and part of what we call "American responsibility," that such often absolutely reactionary substantive imperatives emerge again and again. These days the collective call for a "strong America" that swept Reagan into power is just one such wave of substantive imperatives. All this and several other factors that are codetermining the antinuclear discourse can be expressed in two ways (let alone the simple demagogic exploitation of such and similar facts for the purposes of Soviet propaganda). On the one hand, this all can be regarded as the "natural superstructural result of a capitalist basis." Simple as this might sound, it is totally unacceptable to us. We prefer to see in this complex the *conflict-laden coexistence of capitalism and democracy*, in a country that has regularly experienced powerful democratic-libertarian movements but never in its history an influential socialist opposition.

It is on the basis of worldwide depression, the end of American world hegemony, and the syndrome of American responsibility that one should assess the merits and demerits of the present wave of anti-Americanism being carried by the antinuclear movement with a vehemence unprecedented since the movements protesting the Vietnam War. On balance, one can say that on the one hand they are articulating legitimate grievances, various aspects of the American responsibility (unfortunately very rarely in the form of a coherent theory). On the other hand, this anti-Americanism is not necessarily anticapitalist or Leftist (which is not a critique but certainly a refutation of claims coming from the movement); it is invariably unjust when coupled with an uncritical or even favorable treatment of the Soviet Union; it is not necessarily "progressive" (whatever the measure of "progress" can be) and very rarely moral in the sense of certain fundamental moral values. The fact that present-day anti-Americanism is not necessarily Leftist or anticapitalist can be corroborated in a simple way. If one accepts the characterization of *Der Spiegel*, which speaks of a national unity on the missile question unheard of since 1848, a unity which even allowing for journalistic exaggeration is beyond doubt anti-American, it must be clear that the majority of its participants are not enemies of the capitalist system and certainly not Leftist. European anti-Americanism very often joins the highly problematic traditional Latin American pattern where some of the most reactionary or outright fascist movements, such as Peronism, had a resolutely anti-American edge. Even their vocabulary was full of fulminations against "American imperialism." Anti-Americanism is not necessarily "progressive," for the legitimate articulation of the factors of the American responsibility very often blends, in particular in the British discourse, with more than a touch of conservative cultural superiority of the "old continent" against the "young." Similar symptoms of a French anti-Americanism were very evident in the De Gaulle period. Further, when the anti-American tirades are coupled with a more than suspicious silence about what the Soviet system represents, or when there are global equations, the answer is simple: while all attempts at exporting a particular system and imposing it on others can be condemned, wherever the United States engages in such activity the crime is that it often does not export its own system, while in the case of the Soviet Union the crime is that it always does so. Finally, on the part of Europeans who either had been trampled under foot by Hitler or were forced to trample others in Hitler's uniform, and for whom in both capacities the United States appeared as a major liberator, it is simply not moral to ask why the Americans came here in the first place. (Excepting, of course, the kind of historical consciousness for which modern martyrology commences with the Casablanca conference of Roosevelt and Churchill in 1943, and that does not want to know what had happened before, or after, Casablanca on the German side.)

As a third factor (and cause) of the emergence of the antinuclear movements in this particular historical moment, we have mentioned the disappearance of any reasonable and promising perspective of a "humane," democratic, or (to use Alec Nove's terminology) "feasible" socialism. Obviously, this is a much more limited explanation, because it only affects those who are interested, actively or passively, theoretically or practically, in the transcendence of the present, liberal-capitalist organization of society. The number and breadth of the latter are obviously not coextensive with the antinuclear movement. However, the disappearance of socialist perspectives or hopes has considerably contributed to the political-ideological monopolization of the situation by the antinuclear movement and, obversely, to the Leftist self-abandon to the antinuclear cause almost without reservation. Tragic as it is, the loss of socialist perspectives (at least temporarily) hardly needs any corroboration. Excepting dyed-in-the-wool Stalinists, even those in the antinuclear movement who are apologists of the Soviet system to the point of being hypocritical are no longer infatuated with "real socialism." They can serve its strategic interests for several reasons, but they do not feel the slightest enthusiasm for it. The constantly recurring examples of a necessary capitulation in the face of an overwhelming power in order to survive, the scenes of defeat projected for us by the apostles of unilateralism, tell a longer story about their authors' lucid realism as far as "real socialism" is concerned than they would like to have us believe. On the other hand, since 1968 in Czechoslovakia, not even the ruling apparatus or its "progressive" sections promise us a socialism that would be more humane than the "real one." For the ruling apparatus, "socialism" should no longer be attractive. It should be strong, commanding fear and submission.

*        *        *

Is the antinuclear movement Leftist? Ironically, unambiguous answers in the affirmative are given to this question only by the two extremes of the political diapazon: by what is generally called "the extreme Left" (mostly Stalinist or crypto-Stalinist communists) and the militant Right; in both cases we can suspect vested interests as motives for the answer. The first want to give a clean bill of political health to the new movement, at the same time promoting its incorporation-assimilation by such a recognition. The second intend to unmask the antinuclear movement as a dangerous "Leftist conspiracy." The answers coming from all other quarters would be more reluctant and much more qualified, and for very good reasons. First, the movement organizes itself across classes and political parties. We do not possess any reliable sociological survey of the movement, therefore all statements about its social composition can only be approximate. It seems probable that the backbone is provided by the "middle classes" (with a perhaps almost equal share of university students and housewives); but if we accept participation in demonstrations as qualification, we shall in all probability find workers as well as highly placed public servants and church dignitaries. There are antinuclear movements of which the political character of the party backing them is more clearly decipherable. The Italian movement seems to be a combination of Leftists who have been politically socialized by the Communist Party or some of the New Left groups and pacifist Catholics. In Great Britain, it is reasonable to assume that, ever since the Labour Party embraced unilateralism, the majority of the participants in antinuclear demonstrations belong to the Labour electorate, and that their hard core must have always been Leftist of a kind, although obviously there must be some participants of different persuasion as well. However, absolutely no party physiognomy whatsoever can be ascertained regarding the Dutch and German antinuclear movement (which has nothing to do with the otherwise important fact that the Greens as a party have undergone a severe crisis as a result of Leftist manipulations). To look at the scene from the opposite angle, Leftist parties are generally favorably inclined toward the antinuclear movement, but even this factor does not provide a basis of unmistakeable identification. The Italian socialists are critical, the French socialists are, for obvious reasons, almost hostile, while there are always Tory groups who—because of an anti-American rancor—are ready to toy with the idea of embracing parts of the antinuclear ideology. Parties are also extremely changeable on this question. In 1978, the British Labour Party was still firmly "Atlantic," and on the position of the nuclear deterrent so were the German Social Democrats under Schmidt's leadership (although this position has been slowly eroded in both parties); now the former are the European bastion of unilateralism, and the latter have a highly ambiguous position. Party affiliations therefore cannot very well serve the aims of identification. Nor can ideology, for while the antinuclear movement has worked out its own ideology in a surprisingly short time and distributed it through its travelling emissaries on two continents, it is different from previous political ideologies. The movement (whose structure we are going to analyze) is open; people are not screened when entering it; their earlier, or even parallel, convictions have no bearing whatsoever on their participation in the antinuclear movement. This situation has some advantages and some disadvantages, but at any rate it means that prior or parallel ideologies of the participants cannot serve as an absolute indicator of whether the movement is Leftist or otherwise.

In a way, it is rather the contrary, and in itself much more unquestionable, fact that needs some explanation: why have Leftist parties, some of them immediately, others reluctantly, embraced the antinuclear issue with such emphasis and with so little, if any, reservation? The answer is much less obvious than it seems to be, and it varies from country to country. In Japan, the Hiroshima background created an antinuclear atmosphere beyond political parties that can always be used or exploited for Leftist strategies. In France, the French deterrent as a guarantee against national humiliation, the memory of which does not leave French consensual thinking, has been a national institution beyond parties, from De Gaulle to Mitterand. Even the consistently pro-Soviet French communists are inconsistent as to whether or not to sacrifice it to Soviet political interests. In Germany, the recent antinuclear turn of social democracy is very clearly an opportunist maneuver (regardless of the sincere, and very problematic, zeal of several of its older politicians on this question): they want to ride on the antinuclear tide, partly to get back into power, partly to lead the general nationalist trend. (If one wants to be generous, one would accept Grass's explanation as well: the nationalist vacuum in Germany has to be filled, if not by the Left, then by the Right.) Very often, however, the marriage of a Leftist party and an antinuclear movement costs the former a considerable part of its electorate, as in the British case, where, significantly, a party not noted otherwise for its dogmatism on principles if votes are at issue persists in apparently losing positions. The standard answer (''The left must be with the 'cause of peace' '') is a nonanswer. It is historically untrue, and if the antinuclear movement is about human survival as such, as its partisans want us to believe, then all parties, not just the Leftists, should be antinuclear.

Beyond particular-national explanatory factors, there are some common causes that account for this not entirely self-evident relation, all of them having one feature in common: resignation. The end of the seventies will not be written with capital letters in the annals of European socialism. It was the time of a quite unexpected crisis of the welfare state, in particular in Scandinavia where social democratic parties that had been in government since time immemorial lost power overnight. A similar situation occurred in Great Britain, where the Labour Party, governing only intermittently but correctly regarding itself as the founder of the welfare state, was voted out of power in favor of an ideologically militant Tory politics whose objective was to destroy the welfare state totally and to return to nineteenth-century Manchesterism. While sometimes the social democratic turn toward antinuclearism after defeat is clearly overwhelmingly opportunistic, this is not always the case. Social democratic leaders have understood that a totally depoliticized welfare state is exposed to conservative inroads, and thus they now see that some kind of ideology and political education is needed, and, *faute de mieux*, several of them have picked the antinuclear issue, popular anyhow, as one that seemingly provides a framework of political activism. At the same time, Eurocommunism died a silent but not entirely glorious death, which was an event pointing beyond the inner affairs of communism, having a bearing and impact on the whole of European socialism. Despite many skeptical observers, we still maintain that there was an initial impetus in Eurocommunism that could have resulted in a thorough-going reunification of European socialist parties and movements on a democratic and radical platform, putting a resolute end to lingering illusions concerning the Soviet system, at the same time inspiring a new wave of anticapitalist *élan*. Because of a number of inconsistencies, which many analysts stated at the moment of conception and which have never been overcome, this hope too has failed. What happened is exactly what we had predicted:* Spanish Eurocommunism has lost its peculiar political physiognomy, and almost all of its constituency; French Eurocommunism has been nominally "re-Stalinized"; and Italian communism alone, with its characteristic inconsistencies, has remained the honest social democratic contingent of what used to be Eurocommunism. Of course, the permanent mystery in the latter case is the obscurity concerning the existence of several different parties within one.

The New Left too has been engulfed by the worldwide depression. The latter practically annihilated the basic premise of the New Left: the affluent society which has been approached, analyzed, and attacked by various trends of the New Left with various strategies and philosophical creeds, but the existence of which was common background for all of them. The main reason is simple enough: depression does not provide social space for experiments with alternative life styles; when one has problems meeting mortgage payments, one is not usually concerned with establishing communes. This might not be a "sociological law": in fact, we believe that without an at least partial return to the program of the New Left concerning new need structures, there will be no way out of the present economic tunnel. But it is a social fact that masses and leaders alike have turned toward a more traditional budgetary policy under the burdens of depression. The collapse of the Eurocommunist project has resulted in a relapse into half-Stalinist illusions concerning the social character of the Soviet regime on the part of

---

*In "Fear of Power: A Morphology of Eurocommunism," *Thesis Eleven*, no. 2 (Melbourne, 1981).

communists; in the vacuum, there is no sign of unity, rather that of new divisions. The disintegration of the New Left meant the temporary death of all movements, with the exception of a powerful and unconditionally progressive feminism. In an atmosphere like this, the Leftist embracing of antinuclear movements as a "natural" ground of existence is much more comprehensible.

For a general assessment of the antinuclear movement, a general, if inevitably sketchy, morphology of modern movements must be given. The first characteristic of modern social movements is that they are *transfunctional*. We accept Luhmann's distinction as an at least partially relevant explanatory principle. According to this, premodern societies were stratified, and modern (capitalist, industrial) society is functional (in that it is function within the division of labor that creates strata in modernity, rather than certain functions being allotted to particular preexisting strata). Transfunctionality means, in contrast to such typical and important forms of sociopolitical action as the trade unionist, that the specificity of modern social movements consists of their public disregard of social functions in the spheres of recruitment and dynamics. They do not recruit their followers on the basis of identifying with particular functions while rejecting others in principle, nor do they thematically relate the issues to such particular functions. This very fact establishes the "fluid" or "kinetic" character of movements. Collective actions based on function have their defined locus in the social space, borderlines which they must not (and cannot) transgress. The modern social movement, a transfunctional collective actor, is perforce dynamic in that it has no predefined space but flows over the whole "surface" of society in search of supporters and encounters unexpected ramifications of the issue it has taken as a theme. It is, therefore, transfunctionality that establishes the possibility of contestation.

The second distinctive feature is the *public character* of modern social movements. This feature carries the following meaning. Movements must publicly state their issues and objectives, even their strategy and tactics. In this sense they are radically different from conspiratorial groups cloaked in mystery. Public statement of the entire structure of a social movement, its objectives, strategy, and tactics has become a norm, and it is on the basis of this norm that "manipulators" in a movement can be singled out and politically and morally condemned. The public character of modern social movements further implies that they must investigate all the channels and modes of behavior that can make their issues common knowledge. Their potential in this respect is incomparably more restricted than that of political parties, which aim at parliamentary representation, the supreme forum of public life, or even of trade unions, which, with their strike actions, can command attention about their demands from the whole of society. This explains two facts: the growing number of demonstrations and carnival-like festivities in the public space within the customary modes of behavior in modern social movements, the exaggerated gestures and unrestrained comportment, and the close relationship between movements and media, irrespective of their eventual mutual political mistrust. They need each other. Movements make news; news makes the issues of movements public.

A further important, formal, but at the same time substantive distinctive feature of social movements is that they have no claim, as do political parties, *to dominate the entire personality of their followers.* One could object that such a claim has only been raised by communist parties in their prime. However, even the most loosely organized parliamentary parties can make a similar claim, though in milder form. (For instance, if you belong to a particular party, you are supposed to share a certain vaguely formulated ''philosophy,'' or at least you do not publicly profess the contrary; similarly, certain practical affiliations, ways of life, preferences, and modes of behavior are not tolerated in a given party, or at least they meet with disapproval.) The first consequence of this inability to lay such a claim in movements is that there is no formal admittance to them, in marked contrast to political parties, trade unions, and all formalized associations. To give assent to the goals of the movement in any active form is identical with joining the movement. Further, whereas the movement works out its typical collective forms of behavior, one of which becomes predominant in a more or less spontaneous way, these cannot be formalized and regulated by any statute. The absence of the membership card, admittance fee, or regular membership dues is merely the symbol of a deeper fact: there is no binding discipline in modern social movements imposed by any external authority, only a temporary discipline that the participants accept for the duration of an action. Nor is there an inner censor, a sense of moral commitment to a long-term affiliation. This does not mean that no norms whatsoever apply in modern social movements; just the contrary, solidarity or unselfish dedication of one's time and energies to the common cause are major moral imperatives. But belonging or nonbelonging is a morally neutral matter, and the label of ''traitor'' cannot be attached to those leaving a social movement—more precisely, it would constitute a sign of the incipient "Bolshevization" of the movement.

The fourth distinctive feature of modern social movements is that *they are organized on one issue* or a few issues.* Two counterveiling factors tend to weaken the validity of this statement. In certain cases—the German Greens being composed of ecologists and antinuclear activists constitutes the most striking example—modern social movements combine at their outset related but distinct tendencies. More importantly, complex single issues regularly undergo a "nuclear fission," and several movements emerge from the original. However, there is always a limit. Modern social movements, obeying their inner structural cohesion, cannot claim any totality in social understanding or action. Whereas political parties without a comprehensive program are immediately found defective (and are likely to be completely shunned) by their perceptive constituency, such a total view of society is downright counterproductive for movements, precisely because of their transfunctional character.

The fifth distinctive feature is that modern social movements are *primarily social* and *not directly political* in character and objective. By this we mean, first, that their aim is mobilization of the public sphere; second, that the seizure of power is not one of their objectives. In *The West and the Left* we analyzed the peak experience of the sixties, Paris of May 1968, as precisely such an attempt at the mobilization of the public sphere in a movement of disobedience against the state and the political superstructure, and not as a revolution, premature or otherwise. As far as *nationalist* action is concerned, if it is similar to the Occitanist campaign (Touraine's example in his important *The Voice and the Eye*), it is a movement, for it is in harmony with the general morphological formula of modern social movements; if it is similar to

---

*Alun Chalfont makes the following objection to their characterization as single-issue actions: "There are, nowadays, few (if any) 'single-issue' protest movements. The columns of unilateralist protesters carry banners which proclaim the virtues of every radical cause from Homosexual Rights to Anti-Vivisection. The 'peace women' of Greenham Common, who so outraged the local inhabitants in 1982 with their eccentric standards of hygiene (and contempt for their vaunted environmental conservation), seem to be confused not only between unilateralism and the problem of Cruise missiles, but also between disarmament and 'women's liberation.'" Alun Chalfont, "The Great Unilateralist Illusion," p. 25. We do not find this objection convincing. It is natural that certain movements feel sympathy and solidarity with certain others emerging from a like culture. This sympathy and solidarity does not abolish the single-issue character.

the Sinn Fein/IRA action, it is a political organization taking as its aim the seizure of power (in the sense of swapping national sovereignty). The former type of action, the nationalist movement, shares the fundamental characteristic of modern social movements, their international and imitable character, not because there are Occitans elsewhere but because there exist structurally similar problems.

The sixth distinctive feature is that modern social movements are *discontinuous*. They flare up, eventually lose momentum, and only disappear entirely if the single issue (or few issues) expressed by them reaches a maximum attainable solution within a foreseeable future. The alternative trends are obvious. Either the objective is achieved, or new issues emerge from the initial unitary one and the movements split and diverge; or, within the same movement, new issues are raised, occasionally as a result of a (partial or total) reformulation of the initial goal. The fact that modern social movements have perforce a very low-level organizational framework further contributes to their discontinuous character. For a self-reproducing ideology and an extremely high level of (bureaucratic) organization are needed to keep political associations (above all parties) alive, even when they are no longer active and vigorous elements of the political scene. However, both these elements are structurally absent from modern social movements.

The final distinctive feature of modern social movements consists of their being *a crucial factor in the self-determination of civil society*. This has two aspects. First, modern social movements are not launched by permanent and ongoing institutions (state, parties, churches). Such institutions may lend *a posteriori* support to one or another movement, and they generally do so, but if the movements are launched by them, the suspicion arises that we are dealing with "front" organizations and not genuine social movements. Second, all the aforementioned features, separately and combined, entail the impossibility of having a high-level bureaucratic organizational structure within modern social movements. Transfunctionality, the absence of standing and regularly remunerated bureaucracies, the absence of a binding discipline, the self-limitation to a single-issue character, structural discontinuity, the prevalence of the "social" over the "directly political"—all these exclude genuine high-level organization in modern social movements. In particular, the transformation of social movements into parties is excluded. But what if, despite the stern warning of the theory, movements do grow into parties, as spectacularly occurred with the German Greens? The theory has then every right to insist on Fichte's motto:

"So much worse for the facts." A social movement that shifts its natural space in the public sphere toward the parliamentary benches will see itself, sooner or later, as either a dysfunctional party or a defunct movement. (And this is already becoming visible in the crisis of the Greens.)

At this point, a new question arises: Are social movements structurally democratic? Social movements create, simply by their loose organizational framework, their obvious lack of discipline and indoctrination and training, the impression of a spontaneous entity, as opposed to parties, terrorist groups, or paramilitary organizations. On the face of it, they exude democratic spirit. Further, their very emergence on the European scene (they have always had their place in American history) is clearly due to the general postwar consolidation of liberal systems in Western Europe, a region previously swarming with dictatorships. Nonetheless, the question is justified. Three factors have to be taken into consideration when we prepare to talk about the democratic character of modern social movements in general: their democratic potential in relation to their exterior (the state, the political parties, and the rest of society), their procedural democratism, and their "democratic spirit."

As far as the first factor is concerned, modern social movements are unambiguously democratic in relation to their exterior, and in a three-fold manner. First, the transfunctionality and singlemindedness of modern social movements always raise new questions; they adopt as themes new, previously inarticulated grievances. A typical example is provided by the German Green movement, toward which we have a very critical attitude. Nonetheless, this movement broke through the impenetrable wall of political discourse in Germany, monopolized for decades by the two political giants, the Christian Liberals and the Social Democrats. New issues were raised in sociopolitical debate, issues which simply could not be publicized in the smoothly functioning selective mechanism of the German media, and this occurred because of the pressure applied by the new movement. Secondly, with modern social movements new potentials in action appear on the horizon, and not merely in a strictly political sense. The communal way of life, which has lost ground since but has not disappeared, emerged as a new mass option in the social movements of the sixties, *Bürgerinitiative*, or local municipal action in the European movements of the seventies. Finally, every social movement carries in its being an enormous critical potential, primarily a critique of the standing and permanent organizations of the political sphere. The social movements of the sixties presented a practical (and to some extent theoretical) criticism of the communist parties: those of the late seventies present, ironically, the criticism of the social democratic and Labour parties.

The situation becomes incomparably more complex if we examine procedural democracy in modern social movements. As a rough schematization, modern social movements invariably display a structural-organizational dichotomy between leaders of opinion and militants on the one hand, and followers on the other. This dichotomy does not originate from Michels' famous "iron law of oligarchy" (if it was a law, it was a law of the growth of *parties*), nor is it a result of sinister manipulation. Given the single-issue nature of modern social movements, that they do not claim the loyalty of the whole personality, many "common" participants of these movements may be at least as active politically in another respect as the "leaders" of a social movement. However, these leaders of opinion and militants are not elected, nor are they appointed by an elected body. It is impossible to engage in formal procedures such as elections in the fluid medium of the modern social movement. Therefore, these people steer the movement in a much more undemocratic way than happens in the most bureaucratic political parties. And, let us repeat, this is not a sign of "immaturity" but a structural constant of such movements. (Of course, the reverse side of this undemocratic rule is the extremely limited hold on the whole personality of the participants.) As a result, there is an ineliminable tension in modern social movements between their democratic potential toward their exterior and their inner dichotomy (which renders undemocratic procedure a structural necessity). It is important here to mention that movements, because of their transfunctional character, are rarely centered on the workplace. But if they are, the regular contact between people who know each other, the relevance of the workplace for the questions raised by the movement, develops an action pattern in which the assembly is the overarching element; whereas in movements active in the "abstract public space," it is rather the rally that predominates.

The third factor is democratic spirit. This somewhat elusive term denotes a very real process taking place in all modern social movements: the homogenization of opinions and attitudes from the perspective of the single issue of the given movement, which can occur in a democratic or a very undemocratic way. Homogenization is an indispensable task of a movement, given that people enter into it with heterogeneous worldviews, interests, and functions, due to the movement's transfunctionality. Homogenization is also an incomparably more difficult task for a social movement than for a party, given the structural characteristics enumerated above. It can only occur in two distinct milieus: in a symbolic-iconographic or a critical-communicative culture. Although texts play a significant role in both, one can almost say that the first is homogenized by gestures, chants, and icons, in the form of a pantomime theater, the second by text and discussion, in the form of a psychodrama. By this characterization we do not intend to slight the importance of either of the movemental cultures. People of a penetrating intellect participate by the thousands even in a symbolic-iconographic movemental culture, and "theater" describes a prevalent mode of behavior dictated by a structural necessity: seeking public attention. For want of better channels and in order to capture the media, social movements have to "play their role," chant their slogans in the simplest and at the same time most conspicuous way. They must energetically (perhaps not always consciously) imitate good advertising techniques to make their demands known, their issue public. These modes of comportment are formal requirements of homogenization.

There can be no doubt, however, that the critical-communicative movemental culture has a much greater inclination for democratic homogenization than the symbolic-iconographic culture, as it has the assembly at the pinnacle of its prescribed modes of behavior. This contrast is not identical with that of thought versus feeling. There is no smaller number of shrewd and unfeeling operators in the symbolic-iconographic culture than there are constantly enthusing and unthinking zealots in the critical-communicative one. The latter, however, has a potential that the former does not: the roles are reversible in it. This feature, to which the theory of communication rightly attributes great importance, means in simple terms that during an assembly everyone has a chance to speak, at least in principle. The roles of the speaker and the listener are therefore constantly changing in an assembly, whereas at a rally this cannot occur. Structural necessity notwithstanding, this constellation reduces, if not abolishes, the chances of dialogue, and thereby the democratic and Enlightenment facet of the movement.

In the final analysis, the aforementioned exposes the fundamental structural antinomy of modern social movements. If they are centered upon small groups, the dialogic character, and with it the democratic spirit, can be upheld, but the public and transfunctional character which makes limited action a movement is endangered. If it is focused, exclusively or even in large part, on rallies, the movemental character is preserved, but the democratic spirit, already eroded by the anti-democratic procedural features, will be destroyed. This antinomy can only be weakened, not eliminated. One palliative could be a deliberate staging of *alternative speakers* for all rallies, which will not generate dialogue (or at best will lead to dialogue only among the speakers), but will at least stimulate plurality of thinking. The sad fact is, however, that emotional homogenization in the majority of present-day movements takes place in the form of a greater intolerance than in those of the sixties, in the shape of an attitude almost completely impervious to counterargument.

The new social movements of the eighties operate in a space different from that of the movements of the sixties, with a different *modus operandi*, speaking a different language, generating a different imagery. In a manner of speaking the movements of the sixties started from the social margin, as the overwhelming majority of the public space, and certainly its center, was occupied and organized by political parties and state bureaucracies. From there, the majority of the movements proceeded toward the center of the public space, not to seize power or replace existing political parties, but to create counterinstitutions. A minority deliberately and defiantly remained on the social margin and retained their communes and collective-solitary dreams. This can be viewed as the incapacity of social movements to generate new norms and institutional reforms in a time of legitimation crisis, or it could be regarded as *promesse de bonheur* until the movements have petered out; but the course can hardly be denied. In this course the social movements generally bypassed the power centers residing in both the state and the political parties, due to their anti-authoritarianism and self-imposed abstention from the seizure of power. By contrast, from the outset the new movements of life organize themselves in the center of the public sphere. They do not see themselves as gate-crashers who have to give reasons for their being there; they believe that they address issues of interest to everyone and are therefore entitled to act from the center and have nothing to do with the margin. They change their *modus operandi*; they act as pressure groups and do not intend to create counterpowers and counterinstitutions. They are not anti-authoritarian either. They recognize the authority of political bureaucracies and state agencies, and they intend to use them as instruments for the implementation of *their* objectives: the state is expected to defend the environment, abolish uranium mining, dismantle the nuclear deterrent, ban smoking and the use of dangerous chemicals, oversee the quality of health foods. There is also a change of language spoken in the movements. The "red language" of the sixties was the idiom of de-alienation and anti-authoritarianism; the "green language" of the eighties articulates "pollution" and "contamination" (in both a concrete and abstract sense), the "natural" versus the "artificial," health and life. They have a radically different attitude toward the media. While making headlines, the movements of the sixties were extremely hostile to the media: the manipulation of the masses by television and the press was an article of faith for them. The movements of the eighties start from the assumption that their single issue is everybody's concern, so becoming part of the media program is self-evident for them, and this is a reciprocal process. The changes in the "imagery" follow from the exchange of language. In the sixties, "negative incarnate" was absolute alienation, total manipulation, in a word, 1984; in 1984, it is Nuclear Doomsday. A complementary feature is the shift of the target of criticism from consumerism to productionism.

The transfunctional movement is transcultural as well—there is now an antinuclear cultural field (or cultural potential). If in a different sense, Touraine spoke in his book on movements, *The Voice and the Eye*, of postmodernism. Culturally the antinuclear movements (which have until now only stimulated the profit-sensitivity of Hollywood directors) certainly belong to the postmodernist culture in that they are anonymous—collective, centered on "happenings," and therefore prone to improvisation. An attitude of the "end-of-the-culture" organically follows from their general, "end-of-the-world" outlook. The "end of culture" means in simpler terms the end of closed, self-contained, permanently fixated, and completed art works as paradigmatic individuals. By the same token, the trend triggers the birth of new, "happening-centered" genres. We have termed the typical attitude of the antinuclear militants "pantomime theater," as opposed to the psychodrama of the movements of the sixties, a theater which is accompanied by chanting. The main difference between the two kinds of improvised theater is the emphasis on word and text in psychodrama, on the collectively organized nonverbal act in the pantomime theater. The political psychodrama of the sixties stimulated the fantasies of such radical filmmakers as Godard, Jancsó, Pasolini, and Antonioni. There is a good chance that the antinuclear pantomime will find its artists who will write passion plays, text, and music adequate to their life-feelings.

The antinuclear culture is a *powerful new romanticism*. It is perhaps the first major instance since Jena of the early 1800s (where the project was dreamt and designed by a few isolated men and women of genius) in which romanticism could become, for a historical moment at least, a mass movement. Of course, this is just as much compliment as it is criticism. Marx has correctly emphasized romanticism and liberalism as eternal and recurring extreme poles of capitalism, each of which "explains" the other. In that sense, this romantic contestation for historicity is of utmost significance for understanding the limitations and the implicit-explicit dangers of liberal culture. At the same time, it is not only not an Enlightenment project, but rather its diametrical opposite: *a new romantic religion*. This, of course, needs qualifications, for the assertion does not mean to say that the movement is guided, "secretly supervised," or manipulated by the dignitaries of the traditional churches participating in it; just the contrary, they are an important *minority* contingent in it. Nor does this mean that its participants are overwhelmingly religious (although there is no knowledge as to that, and it would be interesting if we had a deep survey). However, the atmosphere created and carried by the movement is religious in the sense of a *modern* religion. Its God is empty, it is nought; there is no "evidence" sought or gained about it, there is no possible "theology" of the empty God. But the central events in antinuclear romanticism are distinctly religious: Doomsday (nuclear holocaust) and the threatening image of "The Day After"; and, on the other pole, Redemption, The Day When We Shall Overcome. The feeling of transcendence is pregnant and omnipresent: we *must achieve a world "beyond,"* a world which will shine in the eternal light of peace, instead of the gloomy and sinister illumination after the Nuclear Fall, after the Event of our having eaten, once again, superfluously and intemperately from the Tree of Knowledge. The language of antinuclear sermons is almost always evangelizing.

At the same time, antinuclear, new romanticism works out a whole set of relevant and deep-seated critical attitudes toward liberal culture. It is, first of all, a radical criticism of *industrialism*. In its contrasting of the organic and inorganic, *natura* and *industria*, it indeed adopts as themes the grave dangers threatening our whole livelihood. At the same time, with its focus on life, therefore health, the new romanticism of the antinuclear era creates several new habits and rites (the rejection of the synthetic manipulation of the body by drugs, health food, health therapy) and above all a *posterotic attitude*. In contrast to the movements of the sixties, which carried forth sexual revolution, the new romantic movements and the culture surrounding them focus on "body-building" as the sign of life and health, creating thereby a new aesthetic locus, a new potential for a future sculpture (just as their cult of nature creates new chances of a future landscape painting).

However, the *moral* issues in the antinuclear culture have a deeply problematic status. One example, that of *militarism*, will suffice to illustrate this. On the one hand, it is an enormous moral gain when one sees masses of young Germans demonstrating against militarism. This gesture alone signals an end of a martial culture starting with Napoleon and concluding in the valor of World War Two. On the other pole there is the complementary slogan already mentioned: "nothing is worth dying for." This slogan has to be analyzed briefly not just from its political but also its moral function and meaning. Morally speaking, militarism (or martial culture) means the transformation of that which is an option into an imperative: a just war (a war for which there is legitimacy within the martial ethos) must be fought, for life is only a relative value. Otherwise we are not a nation, let alone a "great nation," but just a bunch of cowards and deserters. In an Enlightenment-humanistic culture with a moral equilibrium based on the unity of life and freedom, which therefore accepts the concept of the "just war," this remains an option: a just war *can*, not *must*, be fought. Considerations based on pragmatic aspects of mercy can equally be taken into account. In the "morality" of self-Vichyization, there is a "moral" ban on fighting even a just war. The idea of value has not yet entirely disappeared from it ("Nothing is *worth* dying for," the negative formulation reads), but as "nothing" or "nought" is in the pinnacle of the motto, what remains is an "ethic" of *passivity*, a paralyzing "you must not," an amoral cult of life.

When all this is said, we can set out to analyze to what extent the marriage of the Left and the antinuclear movement is, if not "natural," at least a marriage of convenience. We have mentioned that the new social movements of the eighties, the antinuclear movements (including several pacifist, conservationist, environmentalist trends and groups) are iconographic-pantomimic-postmodern, centered on rallies, symbols, and gestures, not on assemblies, texts, and discourse as were the movements of the sixties.* It has also been stressed that the movements of the eighties are not anti-authoritarian. Being totally open, an extremely positive feature, they have no safeguards against the manipulators of opinion, of those infrastructures over them which,

---

*This is not to idolize the movements of the sixties. We will not forget the scene when Adorno and Habermas were surrounded by the threatening psychodramatic actors who found Adorno a bloodless and socially superfluous classicist; we will not forget the narcissistic but violent Maoism born of the movements of the sixties, amidst the maximum of liberal freedoms; nor will we forget the fact that the terrorist wave too was an offspring of this period. However, the mainstream was assembly and discourse centered, and they appreciated freedom as the central and unquestionable value.

without any authority, and mostly on the basis of self-delegation, fabricate their manifestos, issue their slogans, make their international contacts, give collective statements in the name of all participants of mass rallies, and steer views within the movement.*

What are the features of the level and character of discursive communication in the antinuclear movement? Open discourse on the ultimate chances of a civilization is an almost impossible task; therefore it is appropriate to quote Glucksmann's typology of its possible forms:

> Given human beings with diverse persuasions, spontaneously exclusive of each other, unjust in regard to one another: how can we evade that they should kill one another? Thus formulated, the problem has several solutions. First, one can make a *tabula rasa*, by radically exterminating individual opinions in order to impose a general truth which is indivisible, imperial and, for a start, necessarily terrorist. Secondly, one can attempt at an equilibrium of force by force, of ideas by ideas, and gain from the disorder of individual options an order which is constituted by their antagonisms; while each party plays out his own card, the ensemble will make a fragile edifice. Finally, one can, along with Glaucon and Grotius, ponder a deterrent justice which superposes and imposes itself on the dispersed persuasive injustices. The first solution was held by MacNamara in his bellicose years; he sanctified a nuclear superiority which would establish American law everywhere, even in local politico-military conflicts, for example, in Vietnam. Somewhat later, the second was recommended by Kissinger who had taken the example of the European equilibrium of Metternich and the Congress of Vienna. It is clear that in these two cases the nuclear weapons function in the politico-military game in their capacity of ordinary weapons which are quantitatively the most powerful. It is only a third option that takes into account the new quality of a panoply of deterrent *par excellence* which cannot conquer, only suppress its target. Glaucon had a wide view: he did not identify justice with injustice by dreaming about an overarmament of the just which allows him to gain the upper hand over the unjust by injustice; nor did he imagine, following the pattern of a dialectical genesis, to make injustice the successor of justice with the self-complacency of the Hegelian *parvenu* who transcends his origins by forgetting them (*Aufhebung*). Deterrent justice does not present itself as something good which is separated from, and deflected by an external wrong, prior or ulterior, it maintains itself in the heart of an injustice. . . . It is the repulsion of wrong and by no means

---

*If anyone considers this an exaggerated and biased view of the movements, let us point out that in the brewing crisis of the Greens, friends of Petra Kelly, and Kelly herself, now complain about "Leftist manipulators" who expropriate and misrepresent the views of the Green party and movement.

the hypothetical attraction of a good which founds. . . . the tentative, fragile coexistence between different and potentially hostile mortals.*

It will not detract from the validity and elegance of this skeptical but firmly moral position if we question its awkward and unclear concept: "deterrent justice." The rhetorical language is extremely accurate. Not only does it reject "exterminism" (here illustrated by MacNamara, these days an avantegardist of antinuclear trends); it also rejects what is usually called détente and what is not much more than an equilibrium of force. It also rejects all Hegelian dialectics of justice maintained by injustice, freedom by unfreedom. A tolerable, while not entirely safe and far from amical, coexistence of potentially hostile and mutually dangerous mortals can only be achieved by "deterrent justice." However, and from here we proceed with the argument, justice can only be constituted and upheld in a continuous and domination-free discourse, and it is precisely the latter to which the antinuclear movement is very little inclined, for various reasons. Its constituency has been socialized politically by an atmosphere of fear that makes one sensitive to gestures of panic and excommunication, but very insensitive to arguments. The unilateralist position, an inherent consequence of all attitudes that establish an antinomic structure between life and freedom in general, makes thinking itself unilateral or, in a simpler word, biased. The romantic ideologies embraced by the movement, the apocalyptic-religious contrasts of Life and Death presented in the allegorical manner of passion plays, are the least amenable to rational debate. The organizational framework focused on rallies makes ongoing communicative-critical discourse partly superfluous, partly almost impossible. It is through a mute gesture, namely, absence, that one can display one's disagreement.

It is this inherent hostility of the antinuclear movement to Enlightenment that makes the marriage of the democratic Left and the antinuclear movement not only inconvenient but, one hopes, only a transitory episode. Of course, parting ways with the antinuclear cult will not, and cannot, mean for the Left a removing of the "lessons" of the antinuclear period from the agenda. These lessons are negative as well as positive. Instead of presenting a catalogue, let us just state: no movement or party that is historically creative forgets the results of important periods of its development. But our criticism of the antinuclear movement because of its inherent hostility to the Enlighten-

*André Glucksmann, *La Force du Vertige*, pp. 31–32.

ment project has a primary political importance as well. To act in the spirit of the Enlightenment carries the imperative for a movement to present, honestly and realistically, the expected outcomes of its actions in case its promises come true. And to mention only the main vision flaunted by antinuclear prophets and proselytes alike, everything remaining unchanged, can one seriously believe in the promises made by the antinuclear movement of a "peaceful, nuclear-free, and bloc-free Europe," let alone of such a world?

Finally, two additional factors should be mentioned here. Under the impact of the implicit or explicit (but always inherent) unilateralism of the antinuclear movement (which psychologically must always be supported by a positive view of the Soviet Union), lucidity of thinking about "the dictatorship over needs" becomes more and more blurred. To outdo the West German and American admirers of the "peace-loving" President Andropov (who was also a friend of Western culture because he read Jacqueline Susann in the original and drank whisky), communists, not particularly deeply submerged in the sociological and moral significance of the GULAG, tend to forget even what they had known about this abominable society. More ironically, social democrats, who have historically lived in a permanent dread of being Sovietized, now figure as moderators of "false rumors" about Soviet expansionism. The antinuclear hour is the hour of Great Forgetfulness. It is also the hour of further division, if along new and unexpected lines, instead of unification. French communists and German social-democratic liberals are now in almost perfect harmony in assessing European events, in particular Poland. Both regard Jaruzelski as a blessing in (military) disguise, Solidarity a spoilsport, Reagan a Nazi, and Andropov a moderate. On the other pole, the socialist president of France sees himself compelled to lend support, for strategic reasons, and in defense of the national deterrent, to the German conservative presidential candidate, which is, to say the least, a questionable decision. British Labourite statesmen, for a quarter of a century paragons of "opportunistic class compromise," are teaching radicalism, without genuine inner radicalization, to Italian communists, whose at least verbally vehement criticism of the Soviet Union erodes under the burden of antinuclear competition. Without a doubt, the antinuclear issue has brought some necessary lessons for the Left, but the marriage is one of inconvenience.

# V. The Real Alternatives of Civilization and the Leftist Option

Among other things, the limited "Enlightenment potential" of the antinuclear movement means that it does not articulate the genuine alternatives of Europe (and our civilization in general), but rather confronts us with a Manichean choice between Life and Death. But what kind of alternatives can *we* project for Europe and for human civilization?

The following list seems to be a fair summary of the aggregate of antinuclear recommendations. On top of the agenda there is the demand for a nuclear-free Europe, which is, from a military point of view, tantamount to scrapping all American missiles and abolishing the national French and English deterrents, as well as withdrawing Soviet missiles from East European countries. (We are not aware of any relevant suggestions concerning the banning of Soviet missiles within the USSR. This would be fairly impracticable, and it would hurt the antinuclear sensitivity to national sovereignty.) Ecologist groups extend the concept of "nuclear-free" to the nuclear power plants in Europe; this option, however, has a much smaller constituency within the movement. Next comes the demand for a bloc-free Europe, though there are few elaborations of this proposal. Khrushchev in his time repeatedly toyed with the propagandistic idea of a mutual abolition of NATO and the Warsaw Pact, and he at least took pains to deal with the practical details of this very unlikely event (the simultaneity of the act of abolition, some sort of mutual nonaggression pact between the former participants of the two blocks, and the like). Apart from the postulate, nothing similar has been forthcoming from antinuclear militants: predictive speculation is deemed utopian. (We think that, on the contrary, it would be highly practical in that it would immediately show certain very practical dilemmas arising the moment one sets out to realize a bloc-free Europe.) Not even the intended political status of a bloc-free Europe is spelled out clearly enough: Is it going to be a politically more or less unified and defense-integrated Europe, or rather an aggregate of neutral countries? Even a new concept, that of nonalignment, as contrasted to neutrality, has appeared. Mary Kaldor is one of its advocates, but there is no clear indication in what sense nonalignment is distinguishable from neutrality.* At this point, therefore, we have to ask two questions: Is a nuclear-free Europe possible? And further: Is a bloc-free Europe possible? A nuclear-free Europe is indeed possible if one draws the borderline of Europe somewhere along the Polish-Soviet frontier. For there is not the slightest possibility of inducing the Soviet Union to dismantle at home its own enormous nuclear arsenal; in a way, there is not even a moral legitimation for the Soviet leaders to do so, in their capacity as a national government. We have tried to show elsewhere† what the typical attitudes of Soviet citizens toward nuclear deterrent are; therefore, we can sum them up as follows. The denizens of the Soviet societies live in no great fear of an impending nuclear war. They have never feared American military might;‡ there is as wide a contempt for American valor as there is envy of their socioeconomic system and, above all and unanimously, of their prosperity. People are also fully aware that the West had its, at least

---

*A possible interpretation of the concepts is the following. Neutrality has nothing to do with social system; countries belonging to the same type or cluster of social systems can be, and in fact are, neutral, which simply means in the case of the latter that they make no binding promises to follow the others, the similar ones, in any foreign policy initiative they might make. This refraining does not at all exclude ideological-political sympathies with those whose example the neutral countries do not follow. Nonalignment is, however, a socially competitive concept: it means that the nonaligned country makes efforts to build up a social system different from the prevalent modes of social systems in the world.

†F. Fehér and A. Heller, "On Being Anti-Nuclear in Soviet Societies," *Telos* 57 (Fall 1983), pp. 144–62.

‡This is clearly not meant to imply that fear plays an insignificant role in the Soviet societies; indeed, it plays a key role in the socialization of "Soviet Man." However, it is a fear of a different kind: it is fear of unfreedom (and when this has been internalized, it means fear of freedom as well in several respects). It is fear of omnipotent and punishing authorities. It is fear of waves of mass terror which disappeared with Khrushchev but might return at any moment. It is fear of the whims of punishing gods who can change with one arbitrary gesture one's whole usual pattern of life. It is fear of totally unpredictable economic cataclysms (not crises), a fear not of the future but of the eternal repetition of the present, without a way out.

theoretical, chance, in the immediate postwar situation, to crush the Soviet empire and that it missed the bus. Nor do Soviet "citizens" believe that their leaders would start any headlong rush to the precipice. They consider them to be what they are: ruthless expansionists who grab what they can without risk and never release it, but they also know that they have learned from the master, Yosif Vissarionovich, not to take superfluous risks. However, there are different and very real historical experiences which give food for fear: wars with great land armies, either because of East-West tensions (Korea, Vietnam) or because of the inner conflicts of the Soviet system (the Ussuri war between China and the Soviet Union), and, most recently, the war in Afghanistan (in which the Soviet populace either was or could have been directly involved). These are conventional wars resulting in huge casualties. Quite specifically, there is the same fear of the "Chinese steamroller," which can only be halted with a nuclear threat (or preemptive strike), as there had been for almost a century a traditional European fear of the "Russian steamroller." This constellation imposes the duty on the ruling Soviet apparatus, as a *national* government, not to dismantle its nuclear might (which it would not do anyhow). In the face of this, a nuclear-free Europe can only be achieved *unilaterally*, in other words, through the disintegration of the Western alliance, an American renouncement of any defense obligation for the sovereignty and the liberal system of the West European countries. (This can happen with or without the abolition of the French and English national deterrent; the first seems to be out of question, the second far from being utopian.) We do not think that the disintegration of the Western alliance is a totally unlikely possibility. If victory of a pro-Soviet German nationalism and that of a still unilateralist British Labour takes place simultaneously, the alliance will have, to all practical purposes, ceased to exist.

Is then a bloc-free Europe possible? If it is true that under prevailing conditions Soviet nuclear disarmament cannot be achieved, but will instead result in the symbolic gesture of deploying the missiles within the Soviet borderlines, the disbanding of the Warsaw Pact would be a meaningless gesture for Western Europe from a military viewpoint. Of course, it is not entirely inconceivable that the Soviet leadership will at a certain point again conjure up the Khrushchev proposal and promise the disbanding of the Warsaw Pact in exchange for that of the Western alliance. If they do not intend to lose their tactical shrewdness, they are even likely to do so, should the crisis of the alliance reach a certain estimable nadir. In an atmosphere of widespread self-Vichyization, such a gesture could provoke mass demonstrations with the objective of eliminating the American presence in Europe. Soviet leaders can do so for a very simple reason. It is not the Warsaw Pact that integrates East European countries into the Soviet empire but the other way around: since they have been inextricably integrated into the empire, the nomenklatura can even baptize as an alliance or pact what is in fact an integrated Soviet (Russian) Supreme Command of all military forces of Eastern Europe. Inextricable integration is irrevocable as long as the global system exists, and military pacts can be baptized anew (also in the sense of formal cancellation), but this is irrelevant.* Therefore Europe can become bloc-free only unilaterally, a prospect which is far from inconceivable.

If our analysis is correct and both the nuclear-free and bloc-free character of Europe can only be achieved unilaterally, what prospects does Europe face in a world in which the Western alliance has disintegrated, Europe has unilaterally abandoned its nuclear deterrent, while the Soviet Union has retained its gigantic nuclear arsenal? The obvious answer is that the dependence on, and later gradual integration into, the Soviet system is the most likely alternative, perhaps in the form we tried to describe in an earlier chapter. To refute this, one has to come up

---

*It would be a superfluous detour to analyze in detail what this integration means. In short, *economically*, the relation between the Soviet Union and the East European countries is, as we have analyzed in our *Dictatorship Over Needs*, not one of exploitation, but one of their forcible integration into the global Soviet system in a way that could be economically mutually disadvantageous but which ensures Soviet Russian predominance over them. (Their whole raw-material basis comes from the USSR; switching off the tap would mean that the whole industrial process in Eastern Europe would freeze overnight.) From a *military* point of view, the "national" armies of the Warsaw Pact are integrated into the Soviet-commanded Warsaw system (which remains a *Soviet* army even if the Warsaw facade is removed). Z. Mlynář has pointed out (in mss.) that this integration is ensured by (a) the presence of Soviet "advisers," (b) the Soviet Army units overseeing, i.e., keeping in check, the "national" army units in a complex system of territorial arrangement, (c) the absolute numerical and technological superiority of the Soviet units even in sophisticated *conventional* weaponry, (d) the integration and Soviet supervision of the whole communication system of the "national" armies (from division level onward, all commands and signals are relayed through a system controlled by Soviet experts), (e) the deep penetration of the officer corps by the various Soviet intelligence organizations, which is not identical with what is obviously happening in the West (namely, that a superpower has its informers). For all practical purposes, all leading officers of these "national" armies are Soviet officers as well. Granted this, and further granted that everything remains as it is, why should they not agree eventually to a disbanding of the Warsaw Pact, if it has tactical advantages?

with a totally new conception of the Soviet system.

What if Europe resists Soviet expansion? Before even attempting to answer this question, let us point to a telling fact: as soon as one tries to analyze theoretically the situation advocated by the antinuclear movement, that is, the voluntary dismantling of the European deterrent, we either have to project an infantile view of the Soviet societies (dwelling at length either on the peacefulness of its denizens, who do not have a say in strategic decisions, or on the philanthropy of its leaders), which not even its silliest partisans believe, or we are facing, instead of an idyllic peace, the serious alternative of a ravaging war. And what kind of resistance can the European states mobilize against the combined might of the Soviet Union and its Eastern bloc? (The latter are fairly unreliable armies, of course, but they can be used in exactly the same way the Germans used Rumanian, Hungarian, Italian, and other armies on the Eastern front.) The European resistance can be nuclear, conventional, and "political." The first is logically discarded in the scenario we have to imagine for such an eventuality. What can be said for and against the conventional deterrent? The best that can be stated is that it is no deterrent at all, as far as the Soviet Union is concerned; therefore the war will be short, European capitulation guaranteed, and European cities saved from being ravaged. This, again, is based not on any strategic knowledge, but on theoretical (and commonsense) considerations. First, the numerical superiority of the Soviet (and allied) army in Europe is generally an accepted fact; so is their excellent weaponry, good training, and strategic integration. Even if this is called into doubt by the partisans of a "weak and threatened" Soviet Union, common sense demands that we confront one incontrovertible fact: there would be no point in Western strategists' accepting the traumatic political tensions involved in deploying American nuclear weapons in Western Europe if they did not believe in, moreover, if they were not accurately informed of, such an overwhelming Soviet conventional superiority. Further, the unilateral dismantling of the nuclear deterrent, as every antinuclear theorist will tell us, is based on fear. If this is so, where would reservoirs of courage come from in the face of an eventual Soviet action, when a country is threatened not with all-out nuclear destruction (which, we repeat again and again, serves no Soviet interests at all), but "just" with a Hiroshima, launched against it for purposes of education? (Of course, we are aware that there are authoritative Soviet statements to the effect that they will never make first use of their nuclear weapons; however, to keep this book short we do not intend to list here all the authoritative Soviet statements that have ended up being not entirely true.) Limited nuclear blackmail is a very likely move on the part of an invader who does not want to cause excessive casualties among its own armies, who does not have to fear a nuclear counterstrike, and who sees an enormous prize in its grasp. Would a world that had abandoned its nuclear shield because of fear all of a sudden mobilize sufficient stamina to resist under such conditions? And even without considering limited nuclear strikes, and "only" predicting the clash of gigantic conventional armies with ultrasophisticated weapons, the alternative of a conventional deterrent is hardly attractive, nor is it in conformity with the excessive emphasis on human life so widespread in the antinuclear movement. Some of its partisans praise the conventional deterrent for its capacity to inflict "almost as many casualties" on an enemy as are demanded by a nuclear war. If this is so, where does the antinuclear philanthropy remain? If, as stated by Mary Kaldor, the contrary is the case and a conventional deterrent is no guarantee for the nation that uses it against an eventual, almost complete destruction of its own homeland, in what sense is it then a deterrent? Why dismantle the nuclear deterrent, of which, at least theoretically, one thing can be said; namely, that it promises the avoidance of conflict, not just its successful but costly arrangement? (There is, of course, a straightforward and honest argument to this effect: there is no such thing as a deterrent; an aggressive enemy cannot be stopped with certainty. Therefore let us eliminate the nuclear deterrent because the risks do not justify keeping it, and accept the prospect of great conventional wars. While we disagree with this conception, it is perfectly honest. Though there are good reasons why, it is a pity that we never hear such arguments coming from the antinuclear movement.) When one assesses the arguments for and against the deterrent, however, one must not forget about a further important problem: those who have hitherto campaigned against the nuclear deterrent, suggesting its replacement by conventional weapons, now start their campaign against the latter because they are too expensive. The zeal of self-Vichyization knows no limits indeed.

Another important aspect is also continuously disregarded in such a scenario: what would the United States do when the "conventional deterrent" collapsed, with or without a European Hiroshima? It is far from inconceivable that a desperate, even hysterical, American leadership, in a situation of global instability created by the European collapse resulting from the unilateral dismantling of the nuclear deterrent, would challenge the Soviet Union, and this could only lead to the final clash. There is an at least as likely, if not even more likely, alternative: a new American isolationism (the first symptoms of which are already visible), the American realization of its loss of hegemony, a turn toward developing Latin America, and an alliance with the Pacific countries. But we cannot exclude the first version completely. This being so, the result of the antinuclear triumph would be a genuine, not feigned, atmosphere of Sarajevo.

Do the antinuclear strategists of a conventional deterrent conceive the latter as the separate resistance of national armies or as that of a European coalition? If the first is the case, even people as ignorant in military questions as we are can predict with a degree of accuracy the chances that any single European country stands against the Soviet Union. If the second is the case, the strategists should reveal some of their secrets as to how they would achieve a greater European unity than the one created by the fear of the Soviet system which called the Western alliance into being. The fact is that the disintegration of the Western alliance would inevitably bring inner-European tensions to the surface on a hitherto unheard of level. Tension is even a euphemism. Europe could hardly avoid in such an atmosphere the one thing it has not experienced for forty years: wars between the European states. The Greek-Turkish and Yugoslav-Albanian conflicts are well-known and have already been mentioned here; there is no need for repetition. However, the main factor in a new European constellation would be precisely a Franco-German hostility. Would there be in such a situation any guarantee against a French-German clash other than the ban put on it by the supreme arbiter, the USSR (together with the price a decision would demand)? And even if one declares all this so much of a nightmare, the following question is certainly not unrealistic: On what basis should a European military integration rest? It cannot be nuclear, precisely because such a situation comes about as the result of an antinuclear victory. However, it cannot be entirely antinuclear either, for at least in France there is a national consensus to preserve the *force de frappe*. Any collective and creditable conventional deterrent would demand that an infranational command center could dispose of its member states as it deems fit (including the evacuation of certain national territories if need be). But how could that be achieved without imposing the stronger's will on the weaker, precisely a situation which the member nations resent in the American leadership?

At this point, a question should be immediately raised. In fact, it has been raised: Will President Reagan's missiles protect an eventual Western socialism?* Indeed, the proposition sounds bizarre, but that is no argument against discussing it objectively. As far as we can see, there are four possible answers to the question: First, that this is an impossible proposition, because "despite everything," the Soviet Union still represents some kind of socialism, or because the United States does not tolerate regimes other than capitalist. The two arguments can appear in a combined form or separately. We have nothing to add to our analysis of Soviet society, as far as the first argument is concerned: it is an irrelevant answer for us, because we do not consider the Soviet system to be *any* kind of socialism at all. Another matter, in no logical or actual relation to the first argument, is the second argument; it can be true even if the first is not. Moreover, proponents of the second have considerable historical evidence. The United States used all its political power in the period of the cold war at least to oust communists from Western governments (Italy, France) or, preferably, to outlaw them (West Germany, Greece). Even in this period the American mistrust of social democrats was an important factor in the Western political climate. Up until now, they have tried to block what they regard as the "Marxist threat to the Western alliance" by interfering with other countries' sovereign internal affairs (Vice-President George Bush provoked the indignant reaction of President François Mitterand by his "warning" about the danger of communist ministers in the French cabinet). Even today, they publicly discuss the overthrow of the Sandinista regime in Nicaragua in a manner in which so-called strategic and doctrinaire considerations blend indistinguishably.†

---

*The question has been raised, and only rhetorically answered in the negative, by Axel Honneth and Otto Kallschauer, "Strange Encounter with a Familiar Ghost," *Telos* 56 (Summer 1983). In the same issue, the same question is discussed by Boris Frankel and Jeffrey Herf in the context of whether NATO is a neutral medium or a capitalist anticommunist military agency.

†When we state, and condemn, this unacceptable policy, we do not intend for one moment to join the standard Leftist propaganda about the "free" Nicaragua. Nicaragua is a dictatorship, very mild indeed in terms of Latin American reality, one which at present introduces the usual services Leninist dictatorships generally do in their first period (health service, education, etc.); nonetheless, it is a dictatorship the elite of which promised all sorts of democratic rights when it was fighting the bloody (and American supported) dictatorship of Anastasio Somoza without realizing them when in power. Our condemnation is of a regime that, first, arrogates to a superpower prerogatives we reject everywhere and second, is a democracy but which *in this particular region of the world* has absolutely no right whatsoever to figure as the "protector of democratic rights."

In this respect, the Herf-Frankel controversy deserves some attention, for it was the first discussion of NATO on the Left in terms at least in part other than mere *Schimpfworte*. In a nutshell, Herf's argument was that NATO (and its missiles) can indeed protect the Western Left because NATO is a nonpolitical, neutral agency. Frankel's position is simply that this proposition is laughable. We believe that the truth is somewhere in between. It would indeed be too innocent to accept NATO's neutrality when its former general secretary was a former member of the Dutch Nazi party, when its military commanders and civilian personnel have been extremely carefully (and extremely unsuccessfully) screened concerning their Leftist contacts. In an atmosphere where being (or rather, having once been) even pink, not red, meant being a security risk, the natural atmosphere could be nothing but militantly, hawkishly right-wing. The point is, however, that due to the structure of liberal capitalism, the function and role of NATO are drastically different from those of the structures for the integration of the East European *countries*, and not just their armies, into a Soviet Russian system of interrelationships of which the Warsaw Pact and its organs are but a mere facade. We do not have excessive illusions regarding the respect NATO officers in high-ranking posts feel for the national sovereignty of the single member-countries, but it is not NATO's function to integrate the West *politically* under an American "leadership."* Therefore, the Warsaw Pact system is inseparable from a certain political structure, while NATO is not necessarily inseparable. This also provides an answer to the second argument. No doubt, the American preference is for a Western alliance without Leftists of any kind. But it does not follow from this that Leftist governments of different (if not all) kinds in Europe would be incompatible with the American nuclear umbrella.

The second answer to the original question is that the protection of the Western Left by American missiles is not only a possible option, but it is also an unproblematic one. This has been at least the official (not necessarily the internal) position of several socialist and social demo-

---

*It can be regarded as mere hypocrisy that there was support for the Grenada action on the part of a considerable section of American public opinion, while an almost complete consensus would have stopped any lunatic president who would have experimented with the idea of starting an action against a "disloyal" France that left NATO. There is indeed hypocrisy in this, but the preference (the right to national inviolability) granted to European liberal allies remains a fact. This is the ultimate reason why NATO and the Warsaw Pact cannot be compared, and this is perfectly well-known to those German neonationalists who complain about their "servitude" under American rule.

cratic parties, during the cold war and after. The practical and theoretical background of this uncritical and false position (the most spectacular example of which, until recently, was German social democracy) was the erosion of the concept of capitalism in the party's theoretical framework, its cheap substitution with that of "industrial society," an attitude which was not prepared to see the *problematic* coexistence of capitalism and democracy in American policy, only the beneficial effects of both. This apologetic and one-sided position, of course, prepares the ground for such "Saulus-Paulus" turns with little credibility as we witness these days in West Germany. It also blocks the way of an absolute legitimate radical-social critique of the Western system and the Western alliance, as long as the honeymoon with the United States lasts.

A third possible answer to the initial question is that the protection of the Western European Left by American missiles is possible, but not desirable. It is the duty of the European nations, and within them the European Left, to provide the means of their self-defense. This answer is not pro-Soviet, it is not one that advocates self-Vichyization. It observes the situation with sober realism and can be stimulated by nationalist as well as genuinely leftist considerations. (For instance, the argument can be based on the view that nothing that is not self-attained is of any value.) However, all that has been said about the structural impossibility of an exclusively European initiative applies here as well.

The fourth possible answer to the question (the one we agree with) is that it is not impossible for the American nuclear umbrella to protect the Western Left (in other words, that a West European socialism should come about while the alliance exists). It is, however, only possible under certain conditions. The first would be the emergence of powerful American movements that try to curb the share of the capitalist component in American policy-making in Europe and elsewhere and increase that of the democratic forces. Given that in the United States, in this country *par excellence* of individualism, capitalism is still fully legitimized, this can only be a slow and continuous process but one that cannot be altered by European movements (it is an American task), and one without which the Western alliance cannot in the long run be upheld. The second condition would be the total reorganization of the Western alliance, which means (a) restoration of the full sovereignty of the member countries in the nuclear issue (the "double-key" system); (b) recognition of full sovereignty of all member nations in every respect; (c) total political neutralization of NATO (which means that it should be a military organism of the Western alliance regardless of the politics the single member nations, even all of them, embrace); (d) public *and* secret American renouncement of all strategic plans for a limited nuclear war; (e) acceptance of full nuclear exposure by the United States in case of a threat to its NATO allies; (f) redefinition of the missiles deployed in Europe from "tactical" to "strategic" arms, thereby including them in a future SALT agreement; and (g) acceptance by Europeans of their share in the collective risk as a natural condition of a free contract. The third, fourth, and fifth conditions would involve a change in the concept of the "free world" and in American foreign policy in that they should exclude the use of "unfreedom in defense of freedom," in other words, the excommunication of tyrannies whose only merit is their anticommunist spirit. As these are only the formal prerequisites, and as several other substantive factors (such as a lasting upward swing in the Western economic system) are needed for this situation to come about, here we hold only moderate hopes. Even more moderate are our hopes concerning Soviet readiness for a new concept of détente. Our task here, however, has only been to show what is theoretically possible.

What can the Western Left do for what seems to be the only positive alternative? It can be the proper subject of the new concept of détente. This is no propagandistic slogan. If one pays heed not to Western words (which could be bellicose) but to Western deeds, one can determine an unaltered pattern: after a Soviet act of aggression or oppression, first come a wave of indignant rhetoric and some sanctions, which are lifted on schedule when business interests, powerful lobbies demand it. As the dissident Russian poet Joseph Brodsky correctly said, banks and tanks manage the world, and this was never clearer than in the Polish case, where Western banks (and therefore governments) were interested in the regular payment of interest installments on their gigantic debts, not in the actual situation of a nation. It is only a leftist-democratic consensus that can put freedom ahead of interests. Such a consensus can only be forged by a resolute Western Left, which rejects cold war but is not ready to bargain at the cost of the oppressed nations of Eastern Europe.

What is a "political deterrent"? Interestingly, the idea that with Europeans neither the nuclear nor the conventional deterrent can work has emerged on both the Right and the Left. Raymond Aron was the first to come to the following skeptical conclusion. No one should prepare for a war one is not prepared to fight, he said. Europeans are not prepared to fight a nuclear war for they, unlike the Russians and Americans, who have endless territories, live in a small and easily destructible space and have cities that shelter thousands of years of culture without which the Europeans cannot, and will not, live. Nor are they likely to have success (Aron did not fool himself in this respect at all) with conventional armies against the Soviet Union. He suggested instead the establishment of guerilla armies, armed and trained citizens who would not engage in major battles ravaging the European landscape but would inflict such severe damage on an invader that it would face one of two alternatives: either to deport the whole adult population (in which case the rationale for occupation disappears) or to come to terms with them.* Whatever our objection to this theory, it is certainly no proposal for "self-Vichyization," rather a less peaceful version of the pacifists' Great Refusal. There are similar conceptions among those antinuclear theorists who at least admit that there is a danger that a nuclear-free Europe could be Soviet-dependent and that this is not a commendable perspective. Once again, we are not going to discuss with what technical measure a totalitarian occupying power can "pacify" a population, although these must be no great secrets for those who lived under similar occupation during World War Two or who are in any way familiar with Stalin's methods. However, the option has to face, and is not likely to solve, one fundamental dilemma: the ideology, the ethics, and the general atmosphere of self-Vichyization.† Under certain circumstances people are indeed prepared, even in very great numbers, to put up a staunch resistance. But where are these circumstances? Members of the antinuclear movements (in the same breath that they state that the USSR is weak and threatened) predict an "eventual occupation"; the spirit of *defeatism* is in the very structure of

---

*In our view, the weak link in Aron's argument is that it does not recognize that the deterrent was precisely an instrument to *avoid, not to wage*, a certain type of war. If it is not so felt, this is not the result of the character of the deterrent; it has roots in wider and deeper social factors.

†Let us here make one additional methodological remark to justify the use of the term of "self-Vichyization." The more one ponders the perhaps greatest mystery of World War Two, the French collapse and its aftermath, the more one will come to the paradoxical conclusion that Vichy was *not a result but a cause*. The meaning of this Orphic statement is simply this: had there not been in prewar French society views in wide circles that found their summary in the famous aperçu "better Hitler than Leon Blum," there would have been an almost unanimous French resistance and there would have certainly been no Vichy. "Vichyism before Vichy" was the cause of this political monster and national shame. Similarly, the forerunner of a "self-Vichyization" is the ideology and practice of "better Red than dead."

examples the discussants cite to make their argument convincing;* and defeatism thinks far ahead, beyond the capitulation of armies, and considers already the capitulation of civilians. In his book, Glucksmann quotes General de Bollardière, a person whose civilian courage he otherwise highly esteems. The general suggests to his compatriots that, in the event of an occupation, they do not put up an armed resistance because such resistance will only give birth to new Oradours. What chances does Aron's "political deterrent" stand in such a climate?

An additional consideration places further limitations on the much too sanguine European hopes of an eternal peace based solely on the unilateral dismantling of the European deterrent. This consideration pertains to the proliferation issue. It is an open question whether or not caring for European security alone is indicative of a collective egotism; it is, however, certainly a narrow-minded policy. The knowhow necessary for making the Bomb is public and irrevocable. The raw materials indispensable to it are, with more or less difficulty, available. The temptation for many nations to develop the Bomb is often irresistible whatever the reason, be it because they are threatened, because of the urgings of the poor and starving to blackmail the well-fed and rich, or because of a host of other reasons. All this adds a new perspective to the superpowers' nuclear deterrents which, to the greater glory of our civilization, cannot but be called positive. At the undeniable cost of limiting the sovereignty of others, nonetheless, they keep in check nuclear adventurers, not because they are humane but because this is in their interest. However, this is a constant source of dangerous tension, the explosive character of which is disregarded by the Eurocentric view of the antinuclear movements.

Let us raise the crucial, the ultimate question: What are the genuine alternatives of our civilization *when viewed from the perspective of the antinuclear issue*? We cannot see more than four alternatives. Three of these are catastrophic and the fourth hardly contains great chiliastic expectations. Before enumerating and analyzing them, however, we have to make one general comment. In the second half of this century the whole West, on the Right and on the Left alike, increasingly has experienced a dilemma unknown to nineteenth-century Western humanity: *the disappearance of universalistic panaceas*. This is a politi-

---

*In a December 1981 issue of *Le Monde*, a Nobel Prize–winning French physicist argues in the following telling manner: would a French president be so cruel and insensible as to launch the rockets *in an hour when the German-American defense lines had already been pierced by the Soviet columns*?

cally bipartisan phenomenon, gripping people on both sides of the political diapason, and the increasing vogue of anti-ethnocentrism (fashionable on both the Left and the Right) is just one of the symptoms of this situation. Nineteenth-century liberalism and nineteenth-century socialism, the two great world-views of the West, both possessed the unassailable conviction that they would homogenize the world according to their visions. Their last, deeply problematic offspring, Woodrow Wilson and Lenin, were simultaneous (and the last innerly convinced and sincere) heralds of this ultimate and universal panacea.* If we now disregard expansionist propaganda on both sides, and only face honest convictions, we can no longer see even the vestiges of such universalistic panaceas in the West. Traditional liberalism did not lose faith in its ultimate truth, but it certainly did concerning its might and appeal. An increasing number of liberals view the marriage of liberalism and capitalism with suspicious eyes for various reasons: the crimes of capitalism revolt many just as much as they are shocked by the mercenary spirit of those who are ready to sell out liberal freedoms for profit. While the liberal's confidence in free enterprise is unbroken, doubts concerning whether the world can be homogenized according to the spirit of what they call the "free market" are increasing, if they are not already overwhelming. On the other pole, socialists do not, and to some extent cannot, resign the universality of their project. However, major facts raise grave considerations in all those who possess a modicum of intellectual honesty (and we speak of militants as well as of theorists). The first fact is the emergence of "the dictatorship over needs" in lieu of what they had believed socialism to be. This is a regime that is clearly noncapitalist, which is even anticapitalist, but which is equally clearly not socialist. The second fact is the Sino-Soviet conflict. The first phenomenon makes it unambiguously clear that more than the two Marxist alternatives for modernity exist; therefore, no single universalistic-homogenizing panacea will suffice. The second phenomenon reveals the unexpected lesson that even the mutual transcendence of capitalism in a certain direction and the emergence of identical regimes will not eliminate division and the age-old phenomena of tension and military conflicts from the world. The Western socialist, if he or she is intellectually honest enough, has to face the following dilemma. If the idea of a Western socialism (understood as the radicalization of democracy) is realized (a big "if" indeed, given the many preconditions such

---

*It is more than accidental, in fact it is extremely telling, that Mao Zedong turned toward Lenin as a young student, when he became disillusioned with Wilson.

a realization requires), the question remains open as to what extent it could be a solution for other regions of the world. If this is not the case, will the heterogenity of the world not inevitably trigger the same conflicts humanity has always faced in its history or histories? And if this is so, in what sense is ''Western'' or ''democratic'' socialism anything other than a more or less convenient regional solution, and therefore considerably less than the original project had been? These are questions that remain open for us too for the time being.

On this basis, our skepticism concerning the alternatives for our civilization offered by the antinuclear movement will perhaps become more understandable. It is indeed a sign of skepticism if we view three of these alternatives as totally negative (in the combined sense that they either eliminate humankind or eliminate what we can call human civilization) and list only one that is acceptable and harbors at least some positive potential. The first alternative envisages the collective suicide of humankind, ''exterminism realized.'' This is an unlikely alternative (even if we do not have total extinction of the human species in mind); at least theoretically, however, it cannot be entirely excluded. The second sees the capitulation of one great world system before the other because of the fear of being annihilated, which is an equally negative prospect, whoever the victor might be. This too is hardly a feasible scenario. In principle, it could come about in two distinct ways. Either it would involve an almost total disintegration of the capitalist economy, and a consequent general despair for this alternative to come about in the West, or, in the East, huge revolutions that would topple the power of the ruling apparatuses, revolutions surrounded by Western powers and Western threats or blackmail. Unfortunately, nothing in our anthropological make-up excludes such delightful prospects, but they require too many conditions to be simultaneously fulfilled and hence are very unlikely.

The second logically valid scenario is that one of the power groups capitulates before the other at the beginning of a war in which nuclear weapons have already been used but when the bulk of the population remains unaffected. A third alternative involves universal nuclear disarmament, the continued existence of the social competition between the great parallel systems and all the conflicts that ensue from it. As a result, gigantic conventional wars and the gradual decline of civilization are inevitable. This alternative could come about, but it is still very unlikely as there is not the slightest indication on the part of either superpower that it is willing to relinquish its nuclear arsenal, and such a gesture could only be simultaneous and reciprocal.

The fourth, barely tolerable, alternative is the self-repetitive continuation of the present world constellation, with its tensions, abominable social systems, regionally limited freedoms and "habitable areas," famines, and occasional genocides. It would uphold some hopes as well as recrudescent mass hysteria followed by collective hangovers. In fact, this scenario harbors not one alternative but two. The first is the above: the self-repetitive cycle which, on the one hand, *must* have several limits somewhere, and when these are confronted, one of the catastrophic options could become inevitable. On the other hand, its particularly negative feature is its self-feeding and cancerously growing technical cycles, which waste human energies and potentially increase dangers.* The collective time perception imaginable in such a development inevitably shares a certain kind of "enlightenment fetishism." "Progress in time" is here identical with a quantitatively growing and expanding continuum at a certain point of which a "miracle" must happen (an event not explicable in terms of this continuum) in order that the desired positive result might be achieved. This is clearly demonstrable by the example of such a great scientist and noble man as Andrei Sakharov. In his letter to Western antinuclear militants† he recommends the acceptance of the deployment of missiles, a sacrifice we have to accept "for a while." But, one may ask, what will happen after "a while"? There is no answer to this in the continuum theory of a liberal enlightenment. The romantic protest of antinuclearism does a great service to humanity if it answers with despair, even hysteria, and points to the "end of all times" which will thereby disrupt the continuum, warning this civilization (if only negatively) that its time perception is all wrong, for it does not contain a genuine future but only an "eternal recurrence."

The second inherent course consists of the following steps and measures. It would, first, preserve the nuclear deterrent in the recognition that there exists no other course for keeping the mutual appetites of

---

*We do not want to operate with fetishistic categories; nor do we believe that the arms race is primarily technology conditioned. It is sociologically conditioned, by big business and the vested interests of bureaucracies, and also by expansionist strategies. However, there is an implicit and inherent danger in technological self-perfectionism: as long as things go on as they do now, a more perfect weapon than the existing one can always be invented; the potentials of science are unlimited.

†Andrei Sakharov, "The Danger of Thermonuclear War" (An Open Letter to Dr. Sidney Drell), *Foreign Affairs* (Summer 1983), pp. 1001–16.

the superpowers in balance. It would, secondly, impose a general freeze on the arms race, on scientific research aimed at perfecting weapons (curbing the insatiable curiosity of Faustian man, a price to pay for survival, an important condition which is not entirely without negative consequences). Later, and in an atmosphere of genuine confidence, the present levels of both nuclear arsenals could be reduced, but not beyond a level where the theoretical possibility of mutual destruction exists, otherwise the temptation for one side or the other may reemerge. Thirdly, and finally, it will work out, and set in operation, a new concept of détente. Détente meant with Kissinger the Metternichian mutual (and behind-the-scenes) understanding of the "great powers of the world," a total exclusion of importuning plebeians (and the acceptance of the wishes of public opinion only to the extent consistent with a liberal state), the curbing of all "revolutionary" politics the definition of which is "upsetting the *status quo ante*." This is more than the strategic zero-option offered by the Reagan period, but is self-consciously conservative, cynical, and oppressive. Détente meant with Carter an emphasis on human rights, which is a noble principle, and which certainly promised relief to certain oppressed regions (above all, Latin America), but which is inoperative because this is not the facet on which the Soviet societies can be approached in their totality. (By which we do not suggest cynical deals at the cost of human rights, a question to which we remain unambiguously committed.) A new concept of détente would mean a "merging of interest." The West could find a new field of practically endless investment for its dynamic and expansive economy in the Soviet societies, but it should only do so on the condition that this is reciprocated by a measure of institutionalized freedom (such as those requested in Poland by Solidarity in its initial period). When interests are merged, blackmail and competition are not excluded, but it is highly unlikely that the partners would destroy the field where their common interests are interlocked. This scenario is not theoretically inconceivable; moreover, it would be as strong a guarantee against nuclear war as we could imagine at present, and more than this we cannot hope for. Indeed, any further speculation would take us into the realm of "futurology."

As we are determined not to become either prophets or advisers to the Left, we sum up the lessons for ourselves. The antinuclear intermezzo may be weakening, but it is not over; nor will it totally disappear from the Western context. It is far from inconceivable that its worst lessons will be internalized: its false antinomy of life and freedom, its inherent defeatism, its fetishistic attitude in attempting to solve social problems from their technological end and not the other way around. It is also possible, however, that the Western Left will learn the most important and positive lesson from the movements. The West as it stands now, in a marriage that prostitutes democracy through capitalism, in a situation where democracy does not control reckless industrialism, has less and less of a future. This absence of a future is envisioned in the powerful symbolic image of the nuclear holocaust. Therefore, the enlightenment project has to be recommenced: if there is no future, then one should be created. If there is a future again, it cannot be one of either life or freedom, only their merger, which is the condition of the good life.

# About the Authors

FERENC FEHÉR is currently Senior Lecturer in the Humanities and AGNES HELLER is Professor of Philosophy at the New School for Social Research in New York City. They previously taught at LaTrobe University in Melbourne and before that in Budapest, where they were leading members of the Budapest School. Heller and Fehér left their native Hungary in 1977.

Among Agnes Heller's books in English are *The Power of Shame*, *Everyday Life*, and *The Theory of Need in Marx*. Ferenc Fehér is the author (with T.H. Rigby) of *Political Legitimization in Communist States*. Together Fehér and Heller have written *Hungary: 1956 Revisited* and (with György Markus) *Dictatorship over Needs*.